Beliefs, Bing and Me

The Active Role I Took to Tackle Cancer

By

Gillian Harvey-Bush

New Generation Publishing

Jane,

Hope This helps and makes you laugh in places! You can deal with whatever comes your way.

Love

Gill xx

Dedicated to

Clive and Jackson for your unquestioning support in all that I do, particularly my "weird" stuff and for believing in me. I love you both heaps.

Jennifer and Helen: "Sisters. Sisters. There were never such devoted sisters" (Irving Berlin)

Thank you

To all my good friends for your support and particularly:

Justin Buckthorp for your help, nutritional knowledge, advice and friendship. Oh and those "cheeky little drinks!" I can't thank you enough.

Ali Fuller for the hours we spend sharing and discussing, amongst other things, the "universe" along with our thoughts and beliefs.

Simon Greenaway for the fun, laughter and the many similar life experiences that we share.

Matty Burgess for just being you, making me laugh and responding to things as only you would!

Janey Holliday for your energy and for making me part of your 'revolution' to change women's health and mindsets.

Dr Rima Miller & Henrietta Lewis for taking the time to read the original draft & being honest in your feedback.

Eamonn Holmes for writing the foreword.

And of course to:

Mr Kissin & his team at The Royal Surrey for being such an important part of **MY** team.

Finally to all the people who either knowingly or unknowingly through their teachings and books have influenced me over the last few years to be who I am today.

CONTENTS

Foreword

Gill Harvey-Bush is not normal. I mean that in the nicest possible way. Whether she is in work mode or whether we bump into each other by chance, she radiates positivity and warmth that is impossible to ignore. She is an optimist, friendly, straight-talking and genuine. She is also highly qualified and an expert in her chosen field of coaching, where she works with skill and complete discretion. The term "people person" is something of a cliché but it fits Gill perfectly. She is a people person of the best kind, professionally or in private.

Being diagnosed with breast cancer did not faze her. She simply took her own advice, remained positive, ignored all negative messages (even well-meant), harnessed her techniques alongside those of mainstream medicine and achieved the right outcome.

Gill is far from normal, she is an exceptional person. When she has something to say, it's well worth listening to.

Eamonn Holmes, TV Presenter and Journalist

Introduction

What are my reasons for writing this book? Well, as people heard my story of what I did following my diagnosis of breast cancer they kept telling me I had to write a book to tell others about my very different approach. Everyone who asked me seemed to know someone who they thought would be inspired by what I did.

So many of the women and their families I met whilst undergoing and since my treatment had no idea that there were simple things they could do to help themselves, alternatives to feeling helpless (a feeling which many of the women expressed to me) and leaving everything to the medical profession. I was asked again and again about my approach, beliefs, techniques and — *had I written a book they could buy!*

I am **very** aware that there is a huge number of people (including many close friends and family of mine) whose cancer situations are far more challenging than mine was. However I'd like to think that anyone reading this book will be empowered to do what is right for **them** and what **they** believe in. If my story helps to inspire as well then that is a bonus. I wish to emphasise this was **MY** way of doing it, my approach and my beliefs and it's important you find, adapt or modify what works for you.

I originally wrote this book as "my full story", a much longer and very personal version with every little detail in but decided it would be much more helpful to tell my story with less detail making it more about what I did, how I did it and why I did it. However if you want to read the full story I've still got it as a word document!

So where do I start? When I was diagnosed? Actually when I think about it my story starts a long time before then. I am a very different person now from a few years ago. The "old me" would have had a very different experience of my breast cancer story – in fact the only story to tell would have been a "Woe is me" and "Why

3

me?" lament. I would have worn the Victim T-shirt, with good reason in this case and told everybody I could have told, to enlist as much sympathy as possible at every opportunity. Ultimately I know I would have made it out to be a real drama, appeared to be more "ill" than I was (my mindset would have ensured that was the case) and, if I'm totally honest, would have welcomed (if welcomed is the right word) all the sympathy and attention. Everyone reacts differently so in **no way** am I saying that this is what people diagnosed with cancer or any other illness do, I just know it is what the old me would have done. Thank goodness I've changed. Now I see life from a different perspective of: "I'm not always responsible for what happens to me (although my belief with regards to my cancer was actually that I was!) but I can choose how I deal with it". How did I deal with it? How did I do it? Hence this book and if one piece of information or things I say helps just one person in any way then it was worth writing.

One of the questions I am constantly asked about what I did is, "Ahh but have you always been this positive?" The answer is a definite no, it took work and lots of practice!

To give you some background about how I became far more positive about things, I'll start at the beginning of when I consciously took charge of my life, of who I was and what type of person I wanted to be. I had always considered myself a positive type of person compared to others but I was nowhere near as positive as I am now. How do I know that for a fact? Well, because I can look back at the old Gill and see exactly how she would have reacted to the diagnosis of breast cancer.

CHAPTER 1

The Start of Change

Back in 2003 I was working for Thomas Cook Airlines as Cabin Crew Manager South based at Gatwick. It was a full-on job – early starts, late finishes, travelling all over the place but it brought in a steady managerial salary which was the reason I had gone back to work after having my son Jackson. One Saturday – Jackson was ten years old at the time – I can clearly remember him saying, "Dad and I are going out for a bike ride, Mum, but I know you're too tired to come." He didn't say it in a malicious or accusing way but in a loving, caring tone as if he fully understood what life as a senior manager involved. I had waited a long time to have my son. I was missing out and I knew something had to change.

A few months later I resigned and left in June 2003. I had no idea what I was going to do but managed to get some training contracts. I also started surfing the internet looking at various roles and jobs. It was on one of these occasions that I came across a Life Coaching website. Any form of coaching, other than working with athletes, was very new at the time. So I read with interest and did some more research as to exactly what a Life Coach did. One company offered a two-day taster weekend to coaching. I signed up in March 2004.

Needless to say the weekend following the two-day taster I signed up for the Advanced Diploma (that was all there was in those days – no degrees in coaching).

One of the modules I had to tackle was on Neuro-Linguistic Programming (NLP). I had never heard of it and wondered what on earth we were about to learn! What I did learn about was the power of language and the massive effect it has on us. I knew that finding out more about this would be the next thing on the list when I had completed my coaching course.

I finished the course in September 2004, and Andy, one of my coaching "buddies", had a couple of complimentary tickets to go and see Tony Robbins at the Excel Centre and asked if I was interested in going? I had at least *heard* of Tony Robbins.

Well, I listened to the very American-style delivery of Tony Robbins (not exactly my cup of tea!) but I could appreciate the message he was attempting to get across. I did the famous fire-walk with twelve thousand (yes, twelve thousand!) others and at the time was amazed at myself. The things he said and techniques he used helped me to understand that I was actually in control of my brain and I could have control over my thoughts rather than my thoughts having control over me! Also I realised that the past was exactly that – *the past* – and beliefs could be questioned and changed.

I continued to research into NLP courses and bought a couple of books. I looked at all the various courses on offer and the different ways in which they taught it. Eventually my internet surfing brought me to the Paul McKenna Training website, as it was then. The course they were offering fitted all my criteria and I booked to do it in April 2005. The NLP Practitioner's course was seven days long and I attended it with my now very good friend Justin Buckthorp and a colleague of his Tony Perle.

I have never experienced training or learning like it before. The combination of Paul McKenna, Michael Neill and Dr Richard Bandler, three very different, engaging characters, on stage through the day kept it lively and entertaining. The large number of people on the course was a bonus as it gave you plenty of new "clients" to work with through the week. Phobia Day was later in the week and we were warned that there would be spiders (my particular phobia of forty-plus years) and snakes there. I must admit that I was not looking forward to it and if I hadn't been going with Justin and Tony I may well have skipped that day. However I'm so glad that I didn't miss it as I overcame my phobia and later that day, due to the efforts of Justin and Tony working with me, found myself holding a tarantula in my hand! Words can't describe the feeling that followed and I promptly burst into tears.

I was slowly starting to grasp the immense power of language and how changing one word in a sentence can have such an enormous impact on someone. It's obvious really when you stop to think about it, but mostly we *don't* think about it, but then sometimes the simplest of things often is. We were shown techniques to control our thoughts, shut up those negative voices in our heads, as well as to challenge and change beliefs.

The week was mind-blowing to me. I knew I had merely scratched the surface of NLP but I was already revelling in it.

It was towards the end of the course that one of the assistants approached me and asked if I would be interested in becoming an assistant on Paul's seminars. It was a great opportunity to continue to hone my skills and learn even more from helping others.

It was on my first seminar in March 2006, that I saw Paul McKenna demonstrating a tapping technique called Thought Field Therapy (or TFT for short). I must admit when I saw it being demonstrated the first words that came into my head were "what a load of bollocks!" How can a bit of tapping on various parts of your body help reduce an addictive urge?

I decided to embed the knowledge that I did have of NLP before continuing onto the Master Practitioner course. I practised when working with clients, watching interviews on the TV, listening to conversations whenever I could and used it on myself. I challenged and changed a lot of my own personal beliefs. I became far more aware of the enormous amount of negativity that existed not only around me but also in everyday life. What surprised me was how so many people don't like it when you won't be drawn into their negative view of the world. When you don't agree with them – and it doesn't have to be a major issue – they can become quite angry and argumentative!

You'll know them: you get up feeling great, all is well in your world at that moment in time and within minutes of interacting with them you feel completely drained; or they're the *friends* you dread having to call as you know that by the end of the conversation you'll feel exhausted! Needless to say a few of the "drains" have moved out of my life. A few still remain but that's because they seem to want some of "my positivity" to rub off on them. I keep telling them that they can have their own positivity if they are prepared to work on it for a while. Interestingly as the "drains" move out of my life they've made way for the "radiators". Again you'll be able to identify them: they're the people who always make you feel energised when you've been with them and vice versa. Time flies by when you're with another "radiator." Life in general – the media, TV, newspapers – seem to focus on all the negative things in the world so to counteract it you need lots of radiators in your life!

The more I practised on myself the things I'd learnt, the easier it became to make changes in my life and take real control. I found I was questioning my beliefs and looking at how I'd come to have them. In the process many of them changed or I simply discarded them. I found that the more positive I became the more I seemed to attract positive experiences.

I went on to do the nine-day Master Practitioner course in September 2006. It was as compelling as the Practitioner's course. The three trainers on the course were Paul, Richard and instead of Michael a man called John La Valle.

Throughout this whole period of time I was still busy building my business, training and coaching. I was lucky enough to work with some well-known clients. It was at this point I thought I needed to add something else to my toolkit, and having recently assisted on another seminar with Paul decided to train in TFT. My thought process was "don't knock it till you've tried it!"

In November 2006 I trained to Algorithm level in TFT and very quickly grasped how powerful it can be. I continued to train to the Diagnostic level, became a trainer and finally achieved the level of Optimal Health.

I became very interested in two aspects of TFT: the concept of the energy in our bodies being reversed, hence blocking healing, and the effect of Individual Energy Toxins (IETs) in a person. IETs can be anything that you come into contact with either by touching, inhaling or ingesting. There are some very common ones like wheat, dairy, washing powders, perfumes and toothpaste. The more I worked with clients on reversals and eliminating IETs the more interesting the results became. I would describe myself as a sceptical therapist and have been as amazed as my clients at some of the results that we have achieved simply by eliminating IETs. The changes have been physical or emotional, or both.

I have to make a confession here: I personally have no idea how some of the things I do work. But they *do work.* The main point being that "It's absurd not to use treatments that work, just because we don't understand yet" (Dr Bernie Siegel: *Love Medicine and Miracles*),

Throughout the years I've read many different types of self-help books. I've cherry-picked from them, interpreted them in my head so that they make sense for me, and developed some beliefs from them. I've taken things from the worlds of Coaching, NLP, TFT and elsewhere. I've altered and adapted the techniques and skills I've been taught into something that works for me. (I've listed many of the books I've read and found useful at the back of this book.) I'll share with you what I did when diagnosed with breast cancer, how I did it, and why I did it.

I had read all of these books before I was diagnosed and had no idea when I formed my ideas and beliefs from them just how important and useful they would become. Although I have read many other books since, the main ones I will refer to through this book, giving you my interpretations of them, are: *Love, Medicine and Miracles* by Dr Bernie Siegel, *Reality Transurfing,* Books 1, 2, 3, 4, & 5 by Vadim Zeland and those by Paul McKenna, Dr Richard Bandler and Michael Neill.

CHAPTER 2

The Diagnosis

At the beginning of November 2010 I went to the mobile screening unit for my three yearly mammogram. I had the mammogram and went home not giving it a second thought.

The results arrived in the post two weeks later.

Somehow I **knew** before I even picked the envelope up that it was a recall and I had cancer. I opened the letter, and as expected it was a recall. You get a lot of statistics about how many women are recalled, how many of those turn out to be nothing and how many turn out to be benign. I'm sure the majority of women who get such a letter think they are the unlucky one. As I looked down at the letter I heard a voice in my head say, "There's a reason you've got it, you'll work out what it is and you'll be fine." I know people find this hard to believe but I wasn't worried.

I had been extremely busy through 2010 with work abroad as well as at home and think my unconscious mind knew this was my body's way of saying "Halt! Slow down!" Something I never used to be very good at but am now. I hope it will be a lesson to others to pay attention to what your body is telling you and not to ignore or sweep things away.

> *Worry doesn't change anything and it puts you into a negative mindset, which isn't a resourceful state to do anything from. One of my favourite quotes is: "Worry is like sitting in a rocking chair, gives you something to do but gets you nowhere" (F. Gallagher).*

Or was it just a coincidence?

I believe that there is no such thing as a coincidence and that everything happens for a reason. The reason may not be obvious at the time. I've learnt and built a belief that if I just acknowledge it – *"there will be a reason for this"* – then there always is when looking back from some point in the future. I find that approaching anything in life from this belief makes it much easier to cope with, especially if "*it is sent to try us*". I take a deep breath and say to myself, "Okay, I've no idea what the universe is trying to tell me right now but this is happening for a good reason and one day I'll know what it is."

My appointment time came and I checked in at the reception desk and sat down with my book. There was a real mixture of women there, some with partners, some with friends or family members and several on their own like me. There was the normal selection of waiting room magazines, a coffee machine, chocolate and biscuits for sale, as well as the radio playing quietly.

Eventually my name was called out and the lady explained that she was the radiographer who would be doing my mammogram. You are asked not to question the radiographers over the images as these will be explained when you see the doctor. I followed her to the room and she introduced a trainee radiographer and asked if I minded her being there. I have no problem with people who are training being present – otherwise how do they learn to do their job? She explained that there was an area on my right breast that needed checking. She continued to talk, reassuring me that there are many reasons for the recall and often it was nothing to cause concern. My name and details were confirmed and they brought up the images of the previous mammogram of my right breast on the screen behind me where they were working.

I had been calibrating both radiographers – tone of voice, body language – from the moment I met them, knowing that any little change in any of these would actually tell me a lot about my diagnosis without even having to ask.

To calibrate – to determine true values by comparison with an accurate standard (Chambers Dictionary)

A large part of my training with NLP was to calibrate the person you are working with – listening to their tone of voice, watching for small, minute changes in body language, breathing rate etc. You can learn so much by calibrating people and noticing small changes; that helps you to change your own tone and body language appropriately to help them.

I could see them looking at the new image and could hear the senior radiographer training the other lady. As they spoke about the image there was a change in their body language, tone of voice and the looks between them. The changes were enough, from both of them that it confirmed what I already knew, it was cancerous.

I returned to the reception area and continued to read my book. Eventually I was called through by a lady who introduced herself as Dr Rita McAvinchey and was taken to a consulting room. She explained the reason why I had been recalled and brought up the images from my very first mammogram (taken three years ago), then the recent one, and indicated a very small white patch at the back of the breast, close to the chest wall, literally at the edge of the image, that was present on the most recent mammogram but not on the first one. This was the area that they had taken a further mammogram of today

13

wanting to capture the whole area. She went on to say it could be scar tissue or benign or nothing at all and that in most cases they turned out to be benign. They needed to do a core biopsy to be sure.

Knowing what I then went on to find out I consider myself extremely lucky. If I had been 2 or 3 millimeters further out of the machine when I went to the mobile unit it would not have been discovered. The tumour would have had another three years to grow unabated. Also I was very lucky that the team reviewing my mammograms had actually spotted something.

Rita was telling me in the gentlest of ways, as you would expect of a medical person in this situation. Again call it sixth sense if you want but her whole manner told me that she knew what it was. There had been those very small changes in her, from collecting me from the waiting area to talking about the offending white spot on the image. I stopped her and said that I believed she knew exactly what it was. I explained that I was a coach and complementary therapist with a very positive outlook and I did what I refer to as "weird stuff". So I would really appreciate it if she could give me, with her experience, her best educational guess as to what she thought it was so that I could get to work on it straight away. She paused for a moment, looked at me and then said that she was 99.9% sure it was cancerous.

I know that *thinking* you have it and being told you really do have cancer can have a huge impact. This may sound unbelievable but it really didn't have any impact on me hearing the word *cancer*, and no, I wasn't numb to any emotion either. I felt fine. I just heard myself saying in my head, "Right then, now you know what it is you'd better get on with sorting it out. You always wondered what would happen if a client adhered to all your NLP and TFT techniques so you could tell others about it. Well, who better to test it out than yourself?" Guess I should be careful what I wonder about... wonder what it would be like to be a millionaire...or meet George Clooney?

Rita went on to explain that she was so sure that it was cancer that if the core biopsy came back negative the following week she would want to do another one using the mammogram machine. This would mean that she hadn't obtained a sample using just the ultrasound to guide the instrument to the lump. For that reason she would also refer me straight away to a consultant. If a second biopsy was needed and that came back negative then the appointment could be cancelled. However she was so sure of the result that she didn't want to waste any time.

She said there were three consultants at the Royal Surrey, two male and one female, did I have a preference? I said no, it really didn't bother me but I didn't want a "fluffy" consultant, I'd prefer someone who would just tell me things as they were without any sugar coating. And that the only thing I was allergic to was negativity!

She laughed and said, "I've got just the man for you. You'll get on fine with him. I'll get my secretary to book you an appointment in a couple of weeks and call you on Monday with the details".

As a coach I am always challenging limiting beliefs in my clients.

Not wanting a "fluffy" consultant met with one of my beliefs that I had gained earlier in life from working at a hospital for a range of consultants. One consultant in particular, Mr Jack Slater, frightened the life out of me to start with but I came to really respect and like him. His bark was definitely worse than his bite and although he may not have had the best bedside manner with his patients, underneath his very matter-of-fact *approach was a consultant who cared enormously for them and fought for them every step of the way. I was hoping that I would get a consultant just like Jack Slater. As mad as it sounds I **believed** that I would then get the best care possible. What you believe is extremely important.*

Why Beliefs are important!

Believe – to regard as true; to accept as true what is said by someone; to be firmly convinced (Chamber Dictionary)

A belief – is a feeling that something is absolutely true even though it might be irrational or unproven. Our beliefs are instilled in us from childhood and shape who we are, how we behave and how we see others and the world. Beliefs can be empowering or limiting. We rarely question our beliefs as we are so sure they are true. However beliefs can be changed.

Rita pushed a button for a nurse to come and assist while she did the biopsy. I lay on my left side on the bed while Rita got the equipment ready. All the time she and I were chatting about what I did. The nurse arrived and walked round the bed to face me as Rita explained what she needed to do. The nurse also had what I call "that gentle, caring, understanding tone of voice" as she adopted the "oh dear, are you okay?" approach. Rita immediately told her that I didn't need that and that I wanted a much more direct attitude. I think it is really important to treat people as *they* want to be treated and not as *we think* they should be or how *we* would want to be treated.

Don't get me wrong, I know for some people news like this can be devastating and I admit that it would have been for the "old me", and I would have wanted that sympathetic, knowing tone from a nurse. I would probably have been petrified, running all sorts of images in my head, none of which would have been positive or helpful.

While they were prepping me for the biopsy there were lots of what I would call subliminal hypnotic suggestions coming from them:

- the injection will sting
- as the instrument is inserted it will hurt
- you'll feel pushing
- you'll hear the clicking sound of the instrument as it removes the sample of tissue... etc, etc.

Subliminal suggestions basically tell your brain what to expect without you realising the impact. So if someone tells you it's going to hurt you already believe that it will and respond accordingly. Over the years of using NLP, and assisting on courses I've developed my own personal visualisation of a bubble surrounding me. When anyone gives me a negative suggestion it simply bounces off the bubble. My bubble only lets through positive suggestions that will be helpful to me. My bubble goes everywhere with me. Admittedly there are occasions when I've been caught off "bubble guard" and suggestions or negative things have hit me. As soon as I realise something negative is impacting me I can tackle it and bring up my bubble. I knew that my bubble would need to be strengthened over the coming weeks to withstand all the subliminal suggestions, albeit well-meaning or given as information, that would be coming my way. I knew that I had to counteract these suggestions, in effect to tell my brain something different.

The consulting room was lovely and warm so as I lay on my side I took myself off into a lovely daydream (visualisation). I imagined that I was lying on a golden beach in Barbados, I could feel the warm sunshine on my body, I could hear the waves lapping on the shore and distant voices that I couldn't be bothered to listen to and a long, cool drink in my hand. I told Rita and the nurse where I was and really didn't feel anything throughout the procedure. Rita then asked if I knew anything about NLP. I explained that I was a Master Practitioner of NLP. We had a discussion about it as she had some knowledge of it and wanted to learn more. She was sure it would help her to help patients. She said then that she understood why I had wanted to know exactly what it was.

"What's NLP?" the nurse asked.

We both explained it to her very briefly.

A pad was placed over the hole created by the instrument. The nurse said that it can continue to bleed quite a bit and some people have found that it was still bleeding on their way home. For that reason I was asked to go back to the waiting area for fifteen minutes, then I would be called back by the nurse to check the bleeding had stopped. I made sure I was in my protective bubble and could see the negative suggestions about bleeding bouncing off. I started to visualise my team of helpful plumbers (after all, when you have a leak at home who do you call?), quickly closing off the leak and repairing the area. The fifteen minutes passed really quickly and the nurse was soon calling me through to check the area. She removed the pad, looked at it, then at the site of the wound and commented how little I appeared to have bled.

Hmmm… funny that!

A note about visualisation. Many people will swear that they can't visualise and are rubbish at it. I admit that I used to be one of those people. We can all visualise otherwise we wouldn't be able to operate in the world. For example when I ask you to describe your bedroom you actually have to visualise it to be able to do it. When people used to talk about visualisation I thought it meant you could see things as clearly as if they were in front of you or looking at a photograph. It was explained to me that it doesn't need to be that clear and can be an impression – think of the example of your bedroom, or describing the road you live on. That is visualisation. Some people will tell you they can clearly see things. For those of you like me it's about recognising that you can visualise. I like to look upon visualisation like daydreaming. And anyone who knows me well knows that I can very easily daydream about interviewing George Clooney and describe him in detail! I used many different visualisations throughout my treatment as I saw appropriate to my beliefs.

It was early evening as I left the clinic to drive home. Rush hour had started. As I drove home I knew that I didn't want the world to know and would only tell a few select people who I knew could cope with it in the manner that I wanted, that is to give it no real credence, just to treat me like they would if I told them I had a cold.

19

So it wasn't because I didn't want to tell people that I had breast cancer. I know all the concern would have been well-meaning but it was important to me that the "cancer pendulum" (a belief taken from "Reality Transurfing" by Vadim Zeland) wasn't given any extra energy. It was simply dismissed as no big deal so that I could sort it out without any fuss or bother.

When I got home I told my husband Clive the news, I explained that I didn't want everyone to know and the reasons why. He sat down and just said, "I know that with everything you do, your oogly-boogly stuff, you'll get it sorted. You'll be fine". ("Oogly-boogly" is his affectionate term for all the NLP, TFT and other stuff that I do).

He asked what I would tell our 17-year-old son, Jackson, who was in the middle of studying for his A Levels coming up after Christmas. I knew that Jackson had every faith in what I did, would firmly believe that I could use my stuff to get it sorted and therefore, like Clive, not worry about it. Which of course is exactly what I needed from him: the belief that Mum would be fine so there was nothing to worry about. I explained exactly what had happened and that I would get the results the following week. I had been referred to a consultant and that an operation was likely.

He took it all in and just said, "Mum, I'm not worried because I know with all the stuff you do you'll be fine."

I asked if he had any questions, he said no, he understood. It was the most important thing to me that he wasn't negatively affected with his exams looming. I wanted to mitigate anything that might impact on his results and his dream of going to university to study Aerospace Engineering.

> *It is really important that not only are your beliefs*
> *strong about your outcome but those around you also*
> *believe in what you are doing and have no doubts in*
> *their minds either. It helps create a very positive*
> *energy and environment around you. For me there is a*
> *difference between people "keeping positive" and*
> *"believing beyond doubt" about something.*

So I had cancer. It really is just a word and it's the meaning you give to it that has an impact. I ran my film of the future in my head and saw a lot of positive things coming out of this. The universe was giving me this experience for a reason. I wasn't quite sure what at that moment in time but I knew it would be something good. Life went on as normal – just as I wanted it to. It really was no big deal.

As well as telling both my sisters there were a few other people I did want to tell who I knew would understand fully and be able to offer advice. My friend Ali was aware that I had been recalled to the Jarvis clinic and having herself been through something similar several years ago understood perfectly. She texted to ask how it had gone and I called her back. Ali runs her own business as a complementary therapist and we're both interested in "energy" and what the universe is telling us!

I told Ali exactly what had happened and that I had no idea about consultants or whether St Peter's was better than the Royal Surrey. She immediately said that, knowing me, I should ask for Mr Mark Kissin at the Royal Surrey. She explained that she had seen two consultants a few years ago. The first one she'd seen had a lovely bedside manner. She had wanted a second opinion so had been referred to Mr Kissin. He had more of a "no nonsense" approach, just stated the facts and got on with it, no messing around, *no being fluffy!* She said that he would be perfect for me and was sure I would get on well with him. I explained that it might be too late to request him, as Rita's secretary would be calling me on Monday with my appointment. However I would call the secretary on Monday and see if I could request him as my consultant.

I had talked to Ali about the ideas in the Reality Transurfing books so she was very familiar with the principle of energy attaching itself to things. We chatted on for a while about the "cancer pendulum" and letting it drop or fall through, and who I would be telling. Finally we arranged to meet, as we usually do, for a coffee and chat at our favourite coffee shop in Weybridge, the following week.

There was one other person I wanted to talk to and whose help I knew would be crucial to me preparing my body for what it would be going through in the next few months – my now very good friend Justin. He was busy working abroad for a week so my call to him would have to wait.

As I got ready for bed Clive and I both laughed at the lovely multi-coloured bruise that had appeared on my right breast from the biopsy. We chatted as I needed to be sure that he fully understood how I felt about telling people and that I was already "on the case". It was also important that he understood how I felt about it: that I *didn't hate* my cancer. Why would I hate and want to attack and kill a part of me? I loved every bit of me (well okay, maybe not my spare tyre!) and that included what was now a tumour, but that didn't mean to say that I didn't want to change it. I had created this in my body therefore I firmly believed I could change it and create something different. Over the next few days I would be working out what my body was telling me about what I needed to change. My body was telling me something and now it was time to pay attention and *listen.*

I lay in bed working out what I needed to do.

I had cancer and in a very simple explanation, cancer to me means a bunch of chaotic cells, cells that were out of order. Therefore if they were out of order all I needed to do was bring them back into line with all the other cells around them. A bit like a sergeant-major brings troops into line for a parade, creating a very neat and orderly squad. I remembered one of my favourite old romantic comedy films, *White Christmas,* starring Bing Crosby and Danny Kaye, full of great Irvin Berlin songs including of course *I'm Dreaming Of A White Christmas* and *Sisters.* It was always on at Christmas. I had watched it every Christmas since I was a child and still watch it now on DVD. The film holds a lot of meaning for me as I can clearly recall watching it with my Dad when I was five, curled up on his bed in the lounge with my sisters. He was a big Bing Crosby fan and loved to sing, as did my Mum. It was the last Christmas we had with him before he died in the January.

The characters would be perfect to use for my visualisation. There was the strict General Waverley (who underneath his tough exterior loved his troops) backed up by Captain Wallace (Bing Crosby) and Private Davis (Danny Kaye). I immediately visualised the three of them standing around my chaotic cells and starting to work with them to bring them into order, into a neat squad. There was a lot of work to be done in the next few weeks to get them ready for inspection! I could hear them shouting at my cells, being very strict and not taking any nonsense from them but underneath it all caring deeply about them. It brought a lovely warm feeling inside and made me smile at the thought of the three of them, such different characters, attempting to work together. At the same time I lay my hands on my body to give myself some Reiki treatment. I had trained to Reiki Level 1 out of interest and to help support Ali who was running the course. Little did I know then that I would be using it on myself for a very specific reason. Then I guess I must have fallen asleep.

CHAPTER 3

An Epic Weekend!

Saturday morning I was up early. I had two clients booked in to see me in my office at home, the first one at 8.00am. I don't usually see clients in my office I was only doing it because the clinic I work from had stopped opening on Saturdays and I knew these clients well.

My first client arrived at 8.00am and my working day had begun. Interestingly enough he talked about a friend of his who was a doctor and had been doing some research into cancer. I smiled to myself as the conversation continued and quickly pushed my own thoughts back into the file in my head called "Gill's Crap" so I could concentrate on my client.

As I don't want leakage from one client to the next I use the same visulaisation technique in between clients: I make sure I download my thoughts into their file, close it up and pop it back up onto the shelf in my head before retrieving the next one. When I've finished work I take down my file, open it up and all my thoughts are allowed to re-enter my brain so I can get on with my life!

After lunch it was time for me to pack a case and get ready to leave for Gatwick. I was picking up Paul, one of the co-directors of the Virgin Flying Without Fear course, en route to Gatwick for the flight to Edinburgh. I will never forget that weekend for lots of reasons, not just my diagnosis.

It was really cold when I left home and snow had been forecast for Edinburgh. There had already been a light covering, however it wasn't forecast to be too bad over the weekend. This was encouraging. An important part of the course involves taking the delegates on a flight at the end of the day and bad weather is bad news: it makes nervous fliers more nervous or can result in the flight being cancelled. I collected Paul and as we drove to Gatwick we chatted about what had been happening since we last saw each other. We met up at Costa Coffee (an absolute must for Paul!) with Matt, one of the Virgin crew, who was doing the Cabin Crew bit on the course. Paul was one of the people I was going to tell about my diagnosis but I decided to wait until I had the absolute confirmation at the end of the week and knew the date of my appointment with the consultant. There was another course planned the following weekend in Bournemouth. I could tell him then.

If only we'd known when we left Gatwick what an epic weekend we were in for. Talk about a distraction from thinking about anything else! When travelling with Paul and Matt lots of laughs are guaranteed and this trip was no exception.

We landed in Edinburgh to see snow on the ground and light snow falling. We headed for the hotel and checked in.

Before going to sleep I treated myself with some Thought Field Therapy by clearing my reversals, which involves tapping the side of your hand as if doing a karate chop while saying a little affirmation. I climbed into bed, then placed my hands on my body to do some Reiki on myself. I was now ready to concentrate on my visualisation. There was General Waverley, Captain Wallace and Private Davis all busy working on the new group of cell troops. General Waverley was telling them what a slovenly group they were and how over the next few weeks they would be made into a group of cells to be proud of! I drifted off to sleep.

We were starting early in the morning and there had been quite a snowfall over night. However most people made it and the course started on time. As the morning progressed we all became aware of the steady fall of snow outside the windows but the airline was still saying we would fly. As we were about to finish we had news that the airport had now in fact closed. There was some hope that it would reopen later and we waited another hour or so to see if it would. However it seemed unlikely that the airport was going to open soon and, with the condition of the roads outside deteriorating rapidly, the general consensus of opinion with the delegates was that we finish the course in the room and that they could choose a future course to join in order to do the flight.

The airport closing not only impacted on our course's flight but also meant that our flight back to Gatwick was affected. The terminal was packed in all corners with people spilling out into the snow. Time for a Costa coffee break! We discussed what we could do. We worked out rough timings, from our experience of these situations, and decided we could be back in London by the time a flight eventually landed at Gatwick. So we decided to head for Waverley Station (and that brought a big smile to my face thinking of my lovely General Waverley, busy at work getting his troop of cells into order!).

For anyone who doesn't know Waverley station in Edinburgh, it is at the bottom of a long slope. The bus drops you on the main road at the top and you walk down the hill into the station. Walk? Hardly! That was an understatement, we slipped and slid down the road with suitcases behind us through snow deep enough to get into your shoes. It didn't help that we were also laughing hysterically at each other's attempt to stop ourselves from falling over. And after all laughter is the best medicine!

As we trundled down through Scotland and the North of England we started to think about our arrival time into Kings Cross. Next question was, what time did the trains stop running to Gatwick?

Our epic journey continued. I remember looking out at the night and thinking no one is ever going to believe the last three days I've just had! But actually it had been just what was needed, in a very bizarre way, a weekend full of

26

laughter. I pondered on how other people might have spent the last couple of days having been diagnosed with cancer and thought mine had to be out of the ordinary.

At Gatwick Paul and I said goodbye to Matt and headed for the bus to take us to the long-term car park. I gave Paul a lift home, both of us saying "what an epic" and we hoped the following week in Bournemouth would be better! I finally pulled into my drive at 2.35am but with a huge smile on my face thinking it could only happen to me. I did my bit of TFT and crawled into bed completely shattered but still smiling! I placed my hands ready for my Reiki and checked that my "cell troops" were in training under the watchful eye of General Waverley and Captain Wallace, and fell asleep knowing all was well in my world.

CHAPTER 4

Diagnosis Confirmed

On the Monday morning I rang the secretary to ask if it was too late for me to request Mr Kissin as my consultant. The phone rang but there was no reply. However before I had chance to call again the secretary rang me to say that an appointment had been booked on Thursday 9th December at 2.30pm – with Mr Kissin.

Obviously the doctor and Ali were both of the opinion that Mr Kissin would suit my personality and therefore fit my request for someone who was straightforward, matter-of-fact and not "fluffy" in their approach.

The remainder of the week was spent in the normal way: seeing clients and working on my business. As Christmas was approaching there were the additional things that needed doing in preparation for it. I have a very sweet tooth and love all the Christmas food and treats like chocolate. Since learning the various NLP techniques I still enjoy chocolate but don't have to eat it every time I see some. The only time I did tend to over-indulge, like many other people, is at Christmas.

I had my appointment at the Jarvis Centre on the Friday. It started to snow on and off in Weybridge during the week and we had a very heavy fall on the Thursday night. I had been told to ring the Jarvis in the morning to ensure that my results were back before going for my appointment. I rang around ten to be told that they weren't back just yet but they may well be there by lunchtime, so to ring again just before I was due to leave home.

I went out into the snow to start clearing it. I remember the day clearly, one of those beautiful, crisp, cold, clear-blue-sky days with snow covering everything. I cleared the drive ready to take the car out to go to Guildford. I rang the clinic again. "The results are in" – (I smiled as it reminded me of one of my favourite TV shows *Strictly Come Dancing*) – I could go for my appointment.

The car park hadn't been cleared of snow and cars were parking well away from each other. I followed suit and parked some distance from other cars. I went slipping and sliding through the snow into the now familiar reception area, checked in and took a seat. A lady called my name and I followed her through to a consulting room. She introduced herself as a doctor (I can't remember her name) and explained that normally I would have seen the same doctor as last week except she was snowed in at home and couldn't get to the clinic. We had a brief chat, recapping on what had happened last week and she confirmed that I had a grade two cancer. Cancers are graded from one up to four, grade one being slow-growing, four being very aggressive. She also confirmed that it was very small, only 7mm in diameter and for that reason I may well need a wire inserting to mark it for the operation. This would be explained to me by Mr Kissin. X marks the spot! She asked if I had received my appointment to see Mr Kissin, who was an excellent consultant. ("I bet you say that to everyone regardless of who their consultant is!" said a voice in my head. After all, who wants to hear they have been referred to a mediocre consultant?). Seeing him was the next step and she commented that she knew the only thing I was allergic to was negativity. Mr Kissin would like that.

I couldn't wait to meet this Mr Kissin. Ali had already said he would be perfect for me, Rita had referred me to him and now I was being told he didn't like negativity. He sounded my kind of consultant.

I drove home without trouble. Clive was due to go and play at a gig that evening but I got home in time to tell him that it had been confirmed. No drama, just a statement of the facts. I rang both of my sisters and confirmed it to them and promised to keep both of them posted on the situation.

I had all the "mind" techniques well under way, TFT testing every product that came near me or I was about to consume, and self-Reiki. The only thing left to sort out was my nutrition. Justin was away in South Africa working but due back after the weekend. I was looking forward to talking to him and getting his recommendations. I trust him completely and he knows my body probably better than I do (no, not *that* way!) having trained me in the gym for years.

I had another busy weekend coming up with the Virgin Flying Without Fear course on the Sunday being held in Bournemouth. We still had more snow to clear and as I was shovelling away a very good friend, Simon, was walking past on his way to the station. He stopped for a laugh and a chat. When he asked how I was I told him straight out that I had been diagnosed with breast cancer. His face dropped.

"F**K, Gill!"

The techniques and things I did can be used by anyone for a range of situations from giving up addictions to generally changing to a more positive mindset.

The reason I told Simon, and knew he would understand immediately, is that he went through a similar type of situation a couple of years ago. He was diagnosed with a particular type of brain tumour and had been through far more major surgery and treatment than I was likely to need – I'm glad to say very successfully. When diagnosed, he had also decided to take some responsibility for his outcome. He wanted to ensure he was in the best possible health both physically and mentally prior to his treatment, to compliment what the medical profession would be doing for him. With Justin's

> *help he had worked on his physical health and created his own visualisations. I discovered that, like me, he had not wanted to tell everyone and had only told his immediate family until after he had recovered from the operation.*

In the afternoon I packed my bag and waited for Paul. He arrived, loaded my little wheelie bag into the car and I climbed in. The usual banter started between us as we backed out the drive.

"So what's new then? How's things been with you?" he asked. "Anything happen this week to tell me?"

I knew Paul was one of the people who would be able to react in the way that I wanted so I replied, "Yes, I got diagnosed with breast cancer yesterday."

He looked at me with mouth open and just said, "F**K!" (Funny how that word seemed to be the immediate response when I told people – does it say something about my friends?!)

"That's not quite what I was expecting you to say before we'd even reached the main road!"

We both roared with laughter and I told him that was exactly the reaction I wanted from the people I told. We headed for Bournemouth.

CHAPTER 5

Change of Diet. The "Science" Bit

Justin arrived home and I called him with my news. I told him what stage I was at and asked what I needed to do with regards to my diet. He and I had talked many times about what people were eating and the misconceptions around diets, "good food" and so on.

Justin said what he needed to do with me was make me as healthy as possible and boost my immune system. By doing this my body would be in the best possible condition to deal with whatever it needed to deal with in the coming months. He used a lovely phrase that has stayed with me ever since:

"We need to make all your cells sparkle".

The image of my cells sparkling was a good one, as when he said it I imagined them looking a bit dull, tired and unloved, like silverware in need of cleaning. I asked what I needed to do to give them a polish.

How do you see your cells? Describe them in detail. Are they how you would like them to be? If not then imagine them exactly as you want them to be. This visualisation can apply to anyone and everyone whether they have been diagnosed with something or not.

What I like about Justin is that he looks at the whole person, so we concentrated on treating ALL of me, not particularly the cancer; in fact we hardly mentioned it.

He said that I needed to go back to basics, meaning back to what our ancestors would have eaten. The foods to be eliminated from my diet were:

- processed, refined sugar
- ALL grains, so that included wheat, oats, rice, cous cous etc.
- ALL dairy products
- potatoes

Justin gave me a tip. The easy way to work out if I could eat something was to read the label: if there was anything on there that I didn't recognise or that my grandfather wouldn't know, then avoid it.

These items were in addition to the foods I was already avoiding due to them being Individual Energy Toxins for me, including bananas, tomatoes, broccoli, peas, cashews nuts, blueberries and carrots. I had cut these out a year or so before I was diagnosed so that wasn't a problem. I had also reduced my intake of dairy several years ago, being susceptible to having a "bunged-up" nose, and knowing that dairy made mucus. However I did still have ice cream, strong cheddar cheese (well I was born and brought up in Somerset) and I loved my cappuccinos. I was about to kiss them all goodbye as well. We don't own any scales so the next time I went to the gym I weighed myself, not something I normally do. I was interested to see what would happen to my weight during this time, although weight loss was not a priority in any shape or form – getting healthy was! I hate to admit it but I weighed 78kg. I knew that a much better measurement of weight loss was to measure various parts of your body rather than to rely on scales. When I got home I got the tape measure out and took measurements around my neck, two measurements around my bust, waist, hips, each thigh and calf and wrote them down in a book for reference and comparison later.

The reason people should throw away their scales is that it is not an accurate measurement of what is going on in the body. And to dispel the myth that muscles weigh more than fat isn't exactly accurate. A pound of muscle weighs exactly the same as a pound of fat. A comparison would be a pound of lead weighs the same as a pound of feathers, but the amount of lead needed for a pound is much smaller than the amount of feathers required. The difference is that muscle is more dense than fat and therefore occupies less space!

In this chapter I will attempt to explain the "science" behind changing my diet in a very basic way. I trust Justin enough that I didn't need to know all the reasons why or all the details of the research backing it up. If he says *"Do it"* that's good enough for me. However when I started telling people what I did and the reasons for avoiding certain foods everyone wanted to know why. Telling them "because Justin told me to" didn't seem to be enough. They wanted a more *scientific,* if that's the word for it, reason for giving them up.

I'll give you the research that, to me, makes complete sense and that I believe. I can't emphasise enough in this book that I believe whatever **you** believe will have the most impact on how you approach things.

So here goes...my extremely basic guide to the science!

> *Strong beliefs will be the most significant for you and for those around you, whether they are positive or negative. Which is why it is important to surround yourself with people who believe as strongly as you do in your outcome – without any doubt I, of course, prefer to develop positive beliefs – some of which may seem "whacky" to some people but they are my beliefs and work well for me. Hence not concentrating solely on my breast cancer but working from a complete body-and-mind approach.*

Sugar

Eliminating processed or refined sugar was very interesting. There are all the obvious things like cakes, biscuits, chocolates, cereals and flavoured yogurts to avoid. I never put sugar on anything or in any drinks so didn't consume it that way. However as I started to read labels I realised just how much hidden sugar we do actually eat. Did you know for example it's in just about every sauce, pickle and chutney? Then there are all the foods you would never have thought would contain sugar. And it can be cunningly hidden under a myriad of other names:

Dextrose
Dextran
Maltodextrin
Ethyl maltol
Glucose
Sucrose
Treacle
Golden syrup
Sorbitol

to name a few! A big hint is that anything ending in "-ose" can usually be assumed to contain sugar. Lactose (milk products) contains naturally occurring sugars as does fructose (sugar contained in fruit).

There is a good deal of information and research based around sugar and cancer. The majority of it supports the belief that sugar feeds cancer although I managed to find a smaller amount saying that there is no evidence to support this. It really is up to you what you would prefer to believe and follow. Ultimately it's clear that the excessive consumption of processed and refined sugar is not good for our body and general health.

Sugar is needed to feed every cell in our body, cancerous or healthy. We need simple sugar (glucose) for energy. If we cut out every bit of sugar from out diet then the body will find it from another source such as protein or fat.

This is my very simple understanding for the reason to greatly reduce or limit your sugar intake.

When you eat a lot of sugar your body has to produce a high level of insulin to deal with it. What does insulin do? Well, insulin can tell cells to grow or give them a "turbo-charge" in growth. All the cells in your body grow, divide, die and are replaced as part of the natural process of living. However this also means that the cancer cells get a "turbo-charge" in growth when our bodies produce too much insulin. While we need some insulin to function, too much may encourage cancer cells to grow more and is bad for our overall health. (Ref 1 – 6)

For those of you who would like to look at some research the link between sugar and cancer was first made back in 1924 when Dr. Otto Warburg's paper *The Metabolism of Tumours* was published.

Cancer cells don't die off in an orderly way like normal healthy cells do. When research into cancer cell death was carried out at Duke University, North Carolina, U.S.A., they discovered that cancer cells appear to use a combination of sugar and specific proteins to continue to grow when they should die off. The cancer cells appear to utilise sugar at a high rate that enables them to ignore the cellular instructions to die off.

If the body needs sugar and complex carbohydrates to thrive then what can we do to reduce the amount absorbed? Obviously cutting out excess sugar is the first thing we can take control of. The trick is to eat other things that will help reduce the amount of insulin produced when you eat sugar and carbohydrate. When you eat protein, fat and fibre with the simple sugars the body won't make as much insulin in response to the sugar.

So for example when I eat a piece of fruit I have some nuts with it. The nuts contain protein, fat and fibre which helps keep the insulin in balance. I also prefer to have a piece of fruit rather than a glass of juice, again because the fruit contains fibre (the flesh, if you like) that helps balance out the sugar, whereas pure fruit juice doesn't. A good reason not to drink pure orange juice in the morning!

When I was going through the treatment, and up until my six-monthly check-up, I made sure I avoided any processed or refined sugar one hundred per cent. Now I do occasionally eat sauces and pickles that contain a small amount of processed sugar, but only occasionally. If I want to have some sweetness then I'll add a small amount of organic honey, maple syrup or date syrup, all naturally occurring sugars, or eat a *small* amount of fruit.

Wheat and all other grains!

Eliminating wheat meant eliminating anything made with flour – so out went bread, pasta, cakes, pastries, gravy and sauces. The other grains such as rice, cous cous and oats were also out. I need to clarify that I was eliminating *all* of the grain, not that I was simply giving up the gluten bit. So the gluten-free option was *not* an option.

In came quinoa, a seed that looks exactly like birdseed but when cooked is more like cous cous. I admit when I first tried it I wasn't at all happy, it has a very strange taste. However I found some great recipes and started experimenting. I now really enjoy it either hot or cold. I also eat other seeds like pumpkin and sunflower seeds when I want a snack or I sprinkle them on my yogurt or in salads.

To understand the reasoning behind eliminating grains I have to go back in time and look at our evolutionary path and habits. So here is a very potted history and basic outline of our evolutionary story. Should you wish to know more, feel free to go online and read all the information you can find. In fact I would encourage you to do so, that way you can make up our own mind, as I did find a very small amount of conflicting evidence.

Basically as humans we have been in our current anatomical form as Homo sapiens for the last 200,000 years. We were very much "hunter-gatherers", which meant that we were constantly on the move searching for our food or hunting it down. Gathering food along the way meant that we were only consuming food items that were growing wild or could be hunted. No popping into the local supermarket to get what we wanted or fancied! We were never in one place long enough for us to sow seeds, wait for them to grow and then reap them. In other words we ate a grain-free diet unless we found some "wheat" growing wild.

Much of the research I've viewed states that we didn't eat grains until the agricultural revolution which took place approximately 10,000 years ago. This was the point at which we literally "put down roots" and were able to cultivate crops. There are many reasons why we started to settle in various areas, which allowed us to adopt what we now call agricultural habits. We had also developed the tools and knowledge to process the grains and turn them into flour. It was at this point in our evolution that we started to develop the various grains and eat them in different forms.

There is some research now that suggests that we did in fact eat grains (of the sorghum plant) earlier than 10,000 years ago, as remains of grains have been found from more than 100,000 years ago. Yet this is questioned by other scientists who assert that our ancestors did not have the tools with which to process grains. The "for" and "against" arguments rage on.

Looking at the research, I'm agreeing with Justin and working on the basis that fundamentally we didn't eat grains until around 10,000 years ago, approximately 5% of our evolutionary time. Simply put, physiologically our digestive systems haven't caught up yet and we are not fully able to digest them.

Consuming grains (carbohydrates) is one of the main dietary causes of the production of insulin. When you eat things like bread and pasta the body releases insulin. And we know now what insulin does – *it can tell cells to grow or give them a "turbo-charge" in growth.* There seems to be a bit of a pattern developing here!

But that's not all grains (carbohydrates) do. They also have what is known as a high glycaemic index. The glycaemic index of foods indicates how fast they release sugar into the blood stream. The higher the index the faster they release it. Any foods made from grains become sugar very quickly, especially white rice or products made from white flour like white bread. So now we have yet more sugar being released. And what happens when sugar enters the bloodstream? Yes, you've guessed it – insulin gets released at once to cope with it!

Those lovely grains give us a double whammy of insulin production every time we eat them, whereas vegetables and many fruits, which are also carbohydrates, have a low glycaemic index and therefore release sugar much more slowly into the bloodstream.

To top it all there is even more bad news for us concerning grains. Any grain that is "refined" means that most of the good nutrients that we need have been "refined" out of them. And what, I hear you ask, does that mean, other than the nutrients have gone? Well, wait for it – it means that they simply become even easier sugar to digest! You know by now what that means. It's like giving the "refined" grains their own lane on a motorway straight into your bloodstream.

As I knew I was going to be facing an operation there was yet another reason for giving up grains. Grains contain Omega 6, bad fatty acids very prevalent in the Western diet, which are converted by the body into a couple of things called prostaglandin and leukotrienes. These cause systemic inflammation throughout your body. Even animals that are fed on grain are found to have higher levels of Omega 6 in their bodies that we then consume when we eat their meat.

Obviously the last thing I want when going for an operation (any operation, not just for breast cancer) is an increased level of inflammation in my body. Any reduction in inflammation would mean that my body would be stronger and in a much better condition to deal with the additional healing that I needed it to do. I wanted my body to have the best possible chance of recovering quickly, or as Justin put it I needed "my cells to sparkle". Another reason to give up the grains.

Dairy

Just to clarify this section, when I'm talking "dairy" I mean anything that is made from the milk of a cow. I've had various interesting conversations over what constitutes dairy. Does dairy include goat's and sheep's milk or not? Some would say that it does but for me dairy definitely means anything that comes from a cow. And no, that doesn't include eggs (as someone once asked me), because as far as I'm aware cows don't lay eggs!

I have been drinking goat's milk and eating goat's cheese, butter and yogurt for some time. Having suffered in the past from allergies that caused a runny nose and excess mucus (very attractive in company!) I already knew that reducing dairy was a good idea. Dairy has been found to increase the production of mucus (phlegm) in humans because it stimulates the immune response within the body (that's the response our body creates when it thinks we are ill). Goat's milk does not cause the body to respond in this way. That's a good reason to avoid cow's milk if you are suffering from a cold.

Please note I said "reducing" dairy, not completely avoiding. I still enjoyed my cappuccino or latte when out and ate dairy ice cream, dairy yogurts, as well as the occasional chunk of cheddar cheese. When diagnosed I gave up dairy completely and switched entirely to goat's milk/cheese/yogurt/butter. I had yet to be introduced to the "nut milks" like almond, hazelnut milk or coconut milk.

Goat's milk is closer than cow's milk in composition to human milk, at the molecular level. It is more digestible because the fat molecules are one-fifth the size of those in cow's milk. The larger fat molecules of cow's milk clump together into large globules in the stomach making them harder to digest and metabolise (greater explanation of why this happens further on). Goat's milk contains a preformed vitamin A in the fat that allows it to be easily digested and available to use by the body. In cow's milk the vitamin A must be converted into a usable form by the body. The human body isn't very good at processing any vitamin A we ingest. Approximately 10-30% of what we ingest is absorbed before we excrete the rest. It therefore makes sense to take in "ready to use" vitamin A so we can absorb it before it disappears down the loo!

Goat's milk also contains a more highly evolved cholesterol than cow's milk, which makes it easier for the body and brain to absorb, and also contains a more highly evolved carotene (pro vitamin A) which researchers have found to have cancer-preventing properties.

Goat's milk has an alkalising effect on the body (as does human milk) whereas cow's milk has an acidic effect. Ideally we want to keep our bodies more alkaline than acidic. Excess acidity in our bodies is associated with inflammation (not good for anyone going in for an operation), fatigue, headaches, blood sugar imbalances and excess weight, to name a few. When milk (cow's or goat's) reaches the acid in our stomachs it will clump together into little clusters know as "curd" which can be difficult to digest. A bit like when you add lemon juice or vinegar to milk and it goes into clumps. The difference between the two milks is that goat's milk only forms around 2% curd while cow's milk makes 10% curd for us to digest.

Goat's milk is already naturally homogenised.

> *The definition of homogenisation (according to Chambers dictionary) is "to make (milk) more digestible by breaking up fat globules, to produce (milk) synthetically by mixing up its constituents".*

Homogenised milk is uniform throughout in its consistency so that when it is left to stand it does not naturally separate, with the creamy fat globules rising to the top. When the fat content is naturally more evenly distributed throughout the milk it results in a creamier flavour and texture. Cow's milk has to be mechanically homogenized and there is some evidence to suggest that this process releases an enzyme associated with milk fat (xanthine oxidase) that can penetrate the intestinal wall and enter the bloodstream directly. Some researchers believe this may be the cause of many illnesses including heart attacks and strokes as well as cancer. Of course other researchers deny this. We should bear in mind that the primary reason for homogenising cow's milk is to give it a longer shelf life – a *commercial* reason. As always I stress it's important for you to do some reading of your own, draw your own conclusions and act on your own beliefs.

NOTE: If you can give up all "animal" milk then even better. Since writing the first draft of this book I have started using other "milks" e.g coconut, almond and hazelnut.

Potatoes

Sweet potatoes in the diet date back to 750BC in Peru. However their introduction into Western Europe by Columbus didn't happen until the 1490s. The more common potato was introduced to Europe approximately 80 years later in 1570 but didn't become popular until the 1780s. So we've been eating sweet potatoes for a much longer time.

Sweet potatoes are about twice as high in dietary fibre as the common potato and as a result also have a lower glycaemic index. The glycaemic index, as we saw earlier, is used to measure how quickly blood sugar rises after eating a particular food. The high fibre content slows down digestion and the release of sugar into the bloodstream. By now you all know what happens when you eat sugar: the body has to release insulin. (See Sugar section above)

Sweet potatoes (which are orange inside) are a good source of vitamin C and an excellent source of vitamin A, like beta-carotene. These help to eliminate molecules known as free radicals which damage cells and cell membranes. Studies suggest that eating foods rich in these properties, known as anti-oxidants, lower the risk of developing certain conditions like cancer, particularly colon cancer.

The additional bonus of course is that due to the high fibre you feel fuller for longer, eat less and lose weight! There is always a positive!

Having to actually write down the reasons for this chapter has given me a much deeper understanding (not that Justin hasn't explained it a million times to me!) and made it a lot easier to explain to others who have asked. Some have gone on to change their own diets, removing dairy or wheat, or both, with some interesting results on their health and emotional state.

I went shopping and I started reading labels and was shocked at the amount of things that contained sugar.

It was now the beginning of December and the Christmas foods were in evidence everywhere, with mince pies and chocolates being offered everywhere you went. Being someone with a very sweet tooth and loving the traditional Christmas fare, I knew at some point that I would need to use some of my techniques to help myself.

To be honest, though, I did find it easy to give up most of the foods without using any techniques. After all I had the best motivator going: getting my cancer cells back into healthy ones.

The odd time I was tempted to pick up a chocolate, mince pie, biscuit or a "banned" food, with that voice in my head that says, "Go on, one won't hurt you!" I used one of my techniques: I simply looked at the item I wanted to eat and imagined it crawling with little cancer Pac-Man shapes (that shows my age!) gobbling it up, saying to me, "You eat me and we'll eat you, ha, ha, ha, you eat me and we'll eat you". Alongside that I thought about my son and imagined leaving him motherless. Job done. I no longer wanted to eat it.

I do have a dilemma in that I now know that certain things aren't good for you but my husband and son still want to eat "normally" and it is not for me to force them to eat otherwise. I've changed their diets in subtle ways, for example: we all have goat's milk, cheese, yogurt etc; any bread is homemade and I use rye flour (which contains much less gluten than wheat amongst other differences); processed sugar is substituted or greatly reduced in their favourite recipes. I now use a lot more "Raw food" recipes.

We take most meals together as a family and I didn't eat completely differently from Clive and Jackson, I simply adapted what they were eating and substituted what I could eat. For example, if I was making fish and chips for our evening meal I'd have a piece of tuna instead of fish in breadcrumbs, sweet potato chunky chips sprinkled with something like a chili powder whilst they had normal white potato chips. They might have baked beans but, as I'm currently toxic to tomatoes and therefore tomato sauces, I might have a salad. Instead of a sauce over it I might sprinkle lemon juice and a homemade salad dressing.

Sunday roast was easy. I had the chicken or meat (we only eat organic) and lots of vegetables. If I wanted roast potatoes then I had sweet potato, but no gravy because of the flour in it. For pudding (I always make a pudding on Sunday) Clive and Jackson would have the normal homemade dessert and I'd have some goat's yogurt. For meals like spaghetti bolognese or chili and rice I substituted quinoa in place of the pasta or rice. Once I got used to the change it became easy. I may have had to use another saucepan but small price to pay. After all, it just went in the dishwasher with the others!

The only time eating became a bit more of a problem was when I was "eating on the run". I'm often in London for work or was travelling with the Virgin team around the country, and obviously need to eat. When you avoid wheat and dairy, let alone sugar and potato, you suddenly become very aware of the lack of alternative foods on offer. My train from Weybridge goes into Waterloo where there are lots of food outlets, so you'd think it would be easy to find something. Wrong. They all seem to serve wheat in various forms: sandwiches, paninis, bagels, French pastries, cakes. Even the things on offer in the mini-Marks and Spencers, like the salads, have pasta, grains or potato as a base somewhere in them. The only options seem to be a tub of fruit or a selection from the fruit and nut shop. Luckily if I *had* to eat wheat or diary I wouldn't suffer any of the horrendous symptoms that a coeliac suffers but I can certainly empathise with them when trying to eat out. Of course many places now do gluten-free items, which coeliacs can eat, but I didn't.

I very quickly learnt that, for me, popping into the nearest food outlet for something to eat was not an option. I needed to adopt a new behaviour of being a little bit more prepared and taking suitable snacks with me. A mixed bag of nuts, seeds, raisins, dates and sultanas was easy to keep topped up and carry around in my handbag – just enough to stave off the hunger pangs till I got home. When going away the avocados got packed, in addition to my bag of nuts and raisins, which I found I could add to a salad to make a substantial meal. If I was out for the whole day working in a company I took my own lunch with me, in the winter a small flask of thick homemade soup and / or a salad. The number of times other people have looked at my salad with envy and said how appetising it looked. When I say salad I mean much more than a few lettuce leaves, tomato (which, as explained earlier, I don't eat) and a bit of cucumber. My salads include avocado, raw cauliflower, courgettes, peppers, seeds – anything I fancy, really, topped off with some protein.

I've included some of the recipes I use at the end of the book. However I think it's about time food outlets looked at how many of their products contain wheat and consider widening their range of items.

CHAPTER 6

Mr Kissin and the Process

I was due to see Mr Kissin on Thursday 9th December at 2.30pm in the Royal Surrey Hospital in Guildford. I had decided that I would prefer to go on my own and not make a big deal of it. It was just an appointment where I would find out what next and the treatment that would be open to me. I took my book; we had been warned that there might be a wait as Mr Kissin would spend as much time as necessary with each patient. I checked in at the desk and was directed to the end of the clinic area into another waiting area and told to take a seat there. I walked past a lot of women who were obviously at various stages of their treatment, to the area where I had to wait.

Mr Kissin had been held up and as yet wasn't in the building. They would be running approximately an hour to an hour and a half late. I read my book until eventually my name was called and I followed the nurse into a consulting room. Mr Kissin stood up and introduced himself together with Fia, who was to become my breast care nurse. He was fairly brusque in his manner with a matter-of-fact approach but as he looked at me over his glasses (which he wears on the end of his nose) I liked him immediately because he reminded me so much of Jack Slater, my favourite consultant. He was exactly what I wanted, straight-talking and no "fluffy stuff", someone I could and would trust.

> *It was really important to me to have someone I could trust. If I hadn't felt he was right for me I would have asked for a second opinion or another consultant. It was vital for me to have the belief that he was part of **my** team and working with me every step of the way.*

48

*Note: I saw him working **with me,** which may not seem important but it made me feel more empowered over the process rather than me just doing what he suggested.*

He asked me what I had been told and double-checked that I was very aware that I had breast cancer. It sounded very odd to me to hear myself saying, "Yes, I understand I have breast cancer". I felt as if I was a bit of a fraud being there, after all I wasn't ill and knew that everything would be fine. He wanted to examine me to see if he could locate it.

Now there is one thing that I haven't explained: I'm somewhat prudish and shy about being topless – or bottomless, come to that! You would not find me topless even on a topless beach, for example. But sometimes needs must so I start visualising something different when I have to be examined to stop feeling uncomfortable.

After he had finished examining me he returned to his desk to make notes while I got dressed. I sat down and he explained in full, in his very straightforward way, all the various scenarios with breast cancer, the different types (hormonal or not) and the treatment options. He wrote it all out on a piece of paper and as he discounted each option for one reason or another he crossed them out. At the end we were left with surgery in the form of a lumpectomy, which would be performed in the day surgery unit. As the lump was so small a wire would need to be inserted under x-ray to mark exactly where it was so that when they came to operate they could locate it. The wire would be inserted either the day before or on the morning of my operation.

When they remove a tumour they also take 5mm of tissue surrounding the tumour in all directions. The tumour and surrounding tissue are sent to histology to check that there is a 5mm margin of cancer free tissue around the tumour. If the margin were found to be smaller, then I would need to have another operation shortly afterwards so that they could remove more tissue from the area. Once they were happy with the results the operation would then be followed by an intensive six-week course of radiotherapy and five years on a drug called Tamoxifen.

After my post-operative outpatient appointment I would be referred to an oncologist for the follow-up treatment. There was no sign on the scans of any cancer in my lymph nodes, and he didn't expect to find any due to the small size of the tumour, so chemotherapy would not be necessary. He went on to explain that they would remove the sentinel nodes on my lymph system for testing. If those were clear, as he expected them to be, then I would be able to go home later the same day with a couple of stitches. He gave a really good explanation of the sentinel nodes as being like the first few lights on a Christmas tree: if they lit then you didn't need to check any further, if they didn't then you needed to check along the line.

He had requested a further test on my biopsy to see if my cells were hormone-sensitive or what they call ER-positive.

> *Hormone-sensitive breast cancers rely on the female hormone oestrogen to grow and have proteins called receptors that the hormones attach to. When they come into contact with each other the oestrogen stimulates the cancer cells to divide so the tumour grows. Tamoxifen fits into the oestrogen receptor and consequently blocks the oestrogen from reaching the cells. Or, as he put it, they fit on top of the cell like a tap and turn it off causing the cancer to stop growing or to grow more slowly.*

For that reason he wanted me to start taking Tamoxifen straight away. If the results of the test came back showing that the cancer cells were not hormone-sensitive then Fia would call me and tell me to stop taking the Tamoxifen. He said that cancer cells divide roughly every thirty days so he estimated that mine had probably started growing approximately eighteen months ago. A quick calculation in my head told me that was sometime in 2009.

He asked if I had any questions. I certainly did: I wanted to know if, in addition to the little scar, there would be a slight indentation in my breast after surgery? To my way of thinking, if you're taking a lump of tissue out then there would be a space there so everything would fall in to fill it, hence leave an indent on the outside. How wrong could I be?! He had a very indignant look on his face as he looked over his glasses at me.

His reply was, "Mrs Harvey-Bush," (followed by a sigh) "I take great pride in my surgery and the appearance of breasts. We remove the lump then fold the breast tissue over the area to cover it. You will be left with one, possibly two small scars and no indentation."

He went on to explain again that he would remove the 7mm tumour plus an additional 5mm all the way around it. I immediately had the image of a poached egg in my head, the yolk being the tumour and the white being the surrounding tissue. He said that as my lump was so small I would have a wire inserted prior to the operation to mark the exact place. A case of X marks the spot or, in my case, lump! He also explained that whilst I was under anaesthetic they would inject a blue dye just near my nipple into my lymph system. The reason for this dye was to colour the lymph nodes so that they could find them easily if they needed to. He warned me that I would be left with a slightly blue coloured breast for a day or two post-op.

Now what made that image of a Smurf pop into my head at that point? The things I can visualise!

My lymph nodes would be checked with the sentinel ones being removed if necessary and this would be done through keyhole surgery. The nodes would be checked whilst I was in the operating theatre and, if clear, then that would be it. The other tissue would also be sent for histology and if all the infected cells were well within the 5mm diameter then there would be no need for any further operation and I would be on to radiotherapy. I would know at the end of the day. However if any cells were found too close to the edge of the tissue then I'd be kept in and a second operation would be scheduled to remove more tissue before I went on to radiotherapy. He explained that radiotherapy was like sterilising the whole breast after surgery.

He asked again, "Any further questions?"

Oh yes, I had one very important one: "What happens if, when you come to operate, it's not there?"

He looked up over his glasses and said, "Pardon? What do you mean if it's not there?"

I explained, in the only way I can in a short space of time, that I did this weird stuff that included visualisation and was sure I could change it. Again I got that slightly indignant look over his glasses as he replied, "It will be there, Mrs Harvey-Bush, you haven't got long to work on it before your operation. Granted it may be smaller but it will be there!"

Was that a hint of a twinkle in his eye that I saw?

When he realised that I used visualisation he went on to say, "I'd like you to imagine the Tamoxifen eating up all the cells." He thought about it for a minute then said, "No, what I'd like you to do is imagine the Tamoxifen coming up to a cell, locking on to it and turning it off. As if it was a tap of some description."

> *I decided I could add something like that into my story.*
> *The Tamoxifen would be the soldiers' berets, covering*
> *their heads and stopping them from being different*
> *from my other soldiers. It fitted my belief perfectly so I*
> *was happy to use it.*
>
> *Visualisation is SO useful in so many different*
> *scenarios in life.*

He booked me in for 7th January and finally he said that
Fia would give me more information, take me for blood
tests and so on, and to go away now and have a great
Christmas. He added that after all one in eight women (in
his opinion now heading towards one in six) get breast
cancer and I'd done my bit so I would never need to worry
about it again. My first thought was, "Great reframe, Mr
Kissin," wondering if he would know about NLP reframes.

> *An NLP reframe is: the process of changing the meaning*
> *of a statement or situation; changing the frame of*
> *reference to see something from a different perspective.*
> *"When life deals you lemons – make lemonade!"*

Again he asked if I had any further questions. I had one or
two more, which he answered. He softened and said that I
was to remember that I was not in this alone, that he was
there now and we would get through this together.

I left the consulting room with Fia. That was the last
time I actually saw Mr Kissin until I returned to
Outpatients for the results of my operation. He obviously
saw me in theatre but I didn't see him until a couple of

months later. The medical process and preparation was now truly under way.

Fia took me to a small room around the corner from the main clinic area. She started by talking to me to find out how I was feeling and if I fully understood what was going to happen from now on. She then explained that she would go through everything with me, then take me for the blood tests and to the pharmacy to get my prescription filled.

She opened the pink folder she had been carrying, got all the leaflets out and started to explain each leaflet and circle which bits were relevant to me.

I stopped her.

"I don't wish to appear rude or ungrateful for all the information, Fia," I said. "I totally understand that most women would want to read it all, but I'm not going to read any of it."

She looked a little surprised but then enquired if it was to do with the "weird stuff" I'd mentioned to Mr Kissin. I gave her a brief explanation of NLP and how language can have an enormous impact on people, without them even being aware of it.

The impact of words is magnified in a highly emotional or sensitive situation, which I could imagine most people would be in having been told they have cancer. I continued: the leaflets, whilst giving information on what would happen and what to expect, were actually inputting subliminal hypnotic suggestions. These suggestions can then easily be absorbed and become full-blown beliefs about your condition or recovery.

We are all susceptible to subliminal suggestions – it's one way in which advertisers get us to buy their products. We take in suggestions unconsciously without realising it and respond accordingly.

I went on to say that if I was concerned, or experienced anything I felt was untoward during my treatment, I would tell Clive and get him to read the leaflets to see if it was "normal" for someone going through that process.

By getting Clive to read the leaflets, rather than reading them myself, I wouldn't be exposed to the suggestions about how I should feel!

We had an interesting chat about what I believed and the techniques I used. I told her about the IETs I avoided and the diet changes I had made. Fia looked through the leaflets one by one.

"Okay," she said, "don't read that one... or that one... or that one. Oh dear, not that one..."

She was amazed at the amount of hypnotic suggestions made in the leaflets. By the end the only leaflet that she thought I might want to read was the one for The Fountain Centre, a lovely support area in the hospital. The centre had complimentary therapies available, books relevant to cancer and generally a calm environment for anyone to use who was under treatment. Fia also explained that I would now be entitled to free prescriptions for Tamoxifen as I had been diagnosed with cancer. She would get me the necessary forms to send off and then a card would arrive in the post for me to use each time I needed a prescription.

Fia took me to the Phlebotomy clinic to get my blood tests done. It took them some time to locate a willing vein. The result of which was a lovely bruise! We then headed off to the pharmacy to get my prescription for Tamoxifen filled. Fia had a final word with me saying that she would get the information I needed and pop it in the post, and that she was there if I needed to chat. I wished her a Happy Christmas, thanked her for her help and waited for my prescription to be filled.

Before I went to bed that night I took my first Tamoxifen – having not read the small print inside the packet of course as I didn't want to be susceptible to any suggestions of the "side effects", of which there are many in *any* medication packets!

Life continued as normal, with work and clients as well as the excitement of Christmas approaching. The chocolates and goodies to eat started to appear everywhere and I surprised myself by how easy I found it to avoid eating them. It may sound odd but once I'd said "No thanks" I didn't give them a second thought. By not giving them a second thought I didn't give my imagination the chance to get to work on what they would taste like.

It was on the Monday that I was talking to a friend about Tamoxifen. "Didn't your Mum die from a massive stroke?" she asked.

"Yes, why?"

"I thought Tamoxifen wasn't recommended for anyone with close family who had suffered from strokes."

Oh great! So the cancer wouldn't get me, but a stroke might. How ironic would that be? I came home and went in search of the box with the little paper leaflet that is in all boxes of medication. I decided that this was one leaflet I *should* get Clive to read. Sure enough, under the heading BEFORE TAKING THIS MEDICINE was:

"You should not take or be given Tamoxifen Tablets if: …either you or a close relative are prone to events such as strokes or pulmonary embolism".

Well, I guess I couldn't get a much closer relative than my Mum. Time to get on the phone to Fia for some advice.

After several phone calls with the breast care nurses I was advised that even though they hadn't actually been able to ask Mr Kissin another consultant had advised that I stop taking them until I had seen Mr Kissin again, after my operation. The nurse went on to explain that it wasn't standard procedure to put patients on to Tamoxifen prior to their operation anyway, and that Mr Kissin was the only consultant at the Royal Surrey who did so. I got clarification that I should stop taking it, even though I had only taken four tablets so far, until after my operation. She confirmed, "Yes" and not to worry, it wouldn't do me any harm not to take them for this short period of time. I thanked her. I didn't take any more Tamoxifen.

CHAPTER 7

The Pre-Op Preparations

Things continued pretty much as normal in the run up to Christmas.

I received the letter that week for my pre-assessment appointment, it was for the 22nd December at 10am. The next part of this "journey". However I was so clear in my head what the destination would be that the journey was just something I had to take to get there. I could make that journey miserable for me and everyone around me, but I love travelling so, as you've probably gathered by now, mine was going to be a bit more of a non event, even interesting, as I knew what the destination looked like, felt like and sounded like.

I got up early on Wednesday 22nd December, as I wanted to leave in plenty of time to get to the hospital and park. My pre-assessment appointment was at 10.00am. As I left the house I automatically picked up my book and stuffed it in my bag, prepared for the wait.

I arrived in plenty of time and parked without a problem. Typical! How come when you have plenty of time there is never a queue, but when you're late...? I reported to reception. The lady handed me a form to fill in. I took off my coat, sat down, got my glasses out of my bag and started to complete the form. No sooner had I handed it in and sat back down when a nurse called me through to a small consulting room.

She introduced herself and checked my details: name, address, date of birth etc. She explained what she was going to do today and the reason why they needed to check that I was "healthy" and also not carrying the MRSA virus. Apparently you can be a carrier but not display any of the symptoms. Next thing to be checked was my height and weight, both done fully clothed (including boots!). 5 feet 6 inches and 74.8 kilos. Bearing in mind all my winter layers

I knew that I had lost quite a bit of weight already. My arm was then required to take my blood pressure. It was low to normal – but that's normal for me, if you see what I mean – and then came the blood test. I had been busy visualising a lovely healthy vein presenting itself ready to give blood. The nurse had no trouble in getting the sample that she wanted which meant I didn't get another fine bruise! She asked me to move over to the bed so she could connect me up to a machine that would take a trace of my heart (I presume an ECG) – again fine. Then finally came the swabs required for the MRSA test. She had two long swabs (a bit like large cotton buds), one of which was to stick up my nose and twiddle around a bit and the other to wipe backwards and forwards in the crease of my groin!

She explained that the blood sample and swabs would be sent for analysis and if I were found to be carrying the MRSA virus then I would be informed and my operation delayed whilst I was treated for the virus. If everything was fine then my operation would go ahead as scheduled on 7th January. We wished each other a Happy Christmas and I left the department to head home.

When I arrived home there was yet another letter waiting for me from the hospital. I really was on the treadmill of treatment! This letter, including another information leaflet, was from the Nuclear Medicine department to attend there on the 6th January 2011. It was so they could take the X-rays to mark up my lymph nodes ready for my operation on the following day.

In the letter, following the sentence "Two small injections of a radioactive substance will then be injected into the tumour area and also underneath the areola of the breast" was a lovely subliminal hypnotic suggestion: "A little discomfort may be experienced at this stage". Great! Now I had plenty of time to think about, and interpret in my head, how much was "a little" and what they meant by "discomfort". I decided "a little" meant none at all and the women who had said they felt some had a much lower threshold of "discomfort" than me.

You have to watch out for those hypnotic suggestions, they can sneak in when you're not paying attention to them. Once in, they give the "pendulum" excess potential, or energy, and keep it swinging. That's the last thing I wanted.

Christmas Eve – two weeks to go until my operation. I started to up my intake of water, as I wanted to make sure that all my cells were completely hydrated before I went in for my operation. There is no point in drinking loads of water the day before as it literally goes straight through the body and you end up running to the loo all day. I needed to approach this in the same way as someone training for a marathon.

A tip: when you want to increase your water consumption sip it constantly throughout the day rather than drinking big glassfuls all in one go. That helps prevent the water going straight through you and the "dying for a pee" scenario.

Your cells will absorb more of the water when you take it in slowly but steadily throughout the day. Justin's tip is that you know when you're hydrated, as your pee will be a light straw colour and be completely odourless. Not that I tend to smell my pee, you understand!

I love Christmas Eve, getting all the final preparations done for the next day. Like a lot of families we seem to have our own family traditions at Christmas which include: cutting the Christmas cake on Christmas eve (as no-one seems to want a piece on Christmas Day after a big meal); watching *White Christmas* together (Jackson bought it for me on DVD a few years ago so, just in case it wasn't in the Christmas TV schedule, we could be sure to watch it) while I prepare the veg for the Christmas dinner; and we go to my sister's on Christmas Eve around 5pm to exchange presents and have some supper. This Christmas Eve was no different.

Jackson being a teenager means that we now start Christmas Day at a reasonable hour (as opposed to the middle of the night that anyone with young children will know all about!). We popped the cork on our bottle of champagne for bucks fizz as we opened our presents. I had decided that I would allow myself a glass of bucks fizz and a glass of wine at dinner as well as one mince pie. Other than that, the chocolates, cake, mince pies and other Christmassy food would be for Clive and Jackson. Amongst my presents from Clive and Jackson was the season one DVD set of *Ally McBeal*. Somehow I had missed the series when it was on TV in the late nineties and having got the CD of the music wanted to watch the show. Jackson said that after my op I could come home, sit on the sofa and have an Ally McBeal fest.

Christmas was over far too quickly. The New Year arrived and I continued with my regime of drinking plenty of water and eating the things that were good for me. I saw my clients and went to the gym to make sure my body was as healthy as it could be for my operation and that all my cells *sparkled.*

CHAPTER 8

"X Marks the Spot!"

The first week of 2011 consisted of seeing clients on Tuesday 4th January, Jackson starting back to sixth form on Wednesday 5th, my nuclear medicine appointment on Thursday 6th, operation on Friday 7th. Clive also had a gig on the 8th and Jackson was working his normal shift in Waitrose, so that would be perfect – no time for them to worry about me! On Monday 10th January Jackson was taking one of his big Maths A Level exams so it was important that he had nothing to worry about and that I was there for him.

Thursday 6th January arrived. My appointment with Nuclear Medicine was at 11.30am. As the letter said that I would be there for over 3 hours I took some lunch with me. This included what had become normal for me to carry in my hand-bag: a bag of nuts, raisins and dates as well as some fresh fruit and my trusty bottle of water. I'd treated myself to one of my favourite magazines as I saw this as a great opportunity to sit and read a magazine – a rare luxury for me.

I found my way through the maze of the hospital to the Nuclear Medicine department and checked in at reception. The receptionist checked my weight and height. I found out later that this information is used to calculate how much radioactive substance they need to use – obvious really. I took off my coat, got out my magazine and glasses and sat down.

Eventually a man came into the waiting area and called my name. I gathered up my things and followed him round the corner. He led me to a changing area, with cubicles separated by curtains. He gave me a gown to change into with the instructions to have the opening at the front. He told me that when I was ready just to sit and wait until I was called. I could leave my clothes in that area, as I

61

would be changing back into them after the injections. My first thought when I saw him, being the prudish female that I am, was "Oh no, I hope he isn't going to do the injection!" I banished the negative voice from my head and thought nice things instead.

We all have at least two voices in our head (they are what we call thoughts).

The positive voice praises us and encourages us the other voice is negative and criticises what we do, makes us fearful of things and prevents many of us living the life we want. Once you identify that you have these voices and that they are located spatially in a different place in your head you can actually do something to take control of them, particularly the negative voice. These techniques are covered in Chapter 17.

After a few minutes a lady appeared and called me through to a room. She explained in a bit more detail what had been in the letter and leaflet that I had received. She would administer two injections into my right breast and then I'd have to sit and wait for two and a half hours to give my lymph system time to carry the radioactive material around the breast area into the lymph nodes. I would then be x-rayed to pick up the radioactivity in the lymph nodes and allow her to mark their location on my breast area with a pen. She explained that they might see none under X-ray or they may find a few, but that bore no relevance to my condition whatsoever.

She then went through all my personal detail checks, name, address, date of birth etc. She asked if I had breast implants, to which I said no, these were all my own. She said that it made it easier if a patient didn't have implants, as obviously they wouldn't want to puncture them. She checked which breast it was and then went to the lead box and prepared the injections. She warned me that I might feel some of the cold liquid as she administered the injection. The first injection was done into the breast area and I didn't feel anything – again I was in Barbados enjoying the sun, as I had been when the biopsy was taken. As she prepared me for the second one, just under the areola, she did say that this was the one that women had reported as being painful and stinging. Okay, I don't want that suggestion, thank you. So again as fast as I could I imagined it bouncing off me. I admit the second one did sting very slightly but getting stung by a stinging nettle is far more painful in my book.

I left the consulting room, got changed back into my clothes and headed back round the corner into the waiting area. I read my magazine, occasionally dipping into my bag of nuts and raisins and sipping my water. Lunchtime came and went.

Shortly after 2pm I was called through again and asked to get changed again into a gown with the fastenings at the front. I was then taken into the X-ray room. The young radiographer introduced me to a man already in the room (my prudish heart sank). He checked all my details and then explained that they would take three X-rays all lasting about five minutes. I was asked to get up on the bed of the machine. Gulp! Don't think about it, Gill, just do it. Then I started to laugh to myself as the thought passed through my mind that if I'd have been a Page Three model then this would be so much easier!

I lay down and was asked to place both arms over my head. Now I'm lying completely flat, arms over my head. I can't move or see people coming in but I'm very aware that the door is opening and closing. When everything was checked and I'm in the correct position they all leave the room while the first X-ray was taken. I was only aware of some voices chatting and the noises in the room. After a few minutes one of the men reappeared, moved the machine to a forty-five degree angle over me, checked the position and that I'm okay, then disappeared again to take the remaining X-rays.

When the X-rays were finished the senior radiographer, the one who had given me my injections, appeared to my left and explained that she was now going to mark me up. She explained that she would be using a cobalt pen to locate each sentinel node by looking at the computer. As she found each node she used a permanent marker pen to put a cross on each one she found. The young radiographer came back to watch what was happening and commented that she had never seen so many nodes. The senior radiographer agreed with her that there was a long string of them and it was rare to see so many. After what felt like ages I was marked up: seven nodes in total, one node above my breast, five down the side by my arm and one underneath. She then went and got some cotton wool balls and sticky tape and covered them up one by one to protect my clothes from staining. She then told me I could remove the cotton wool when I got home and it would be okay to shower in the morning as long as I patted the crosses dry.

I went back to the cubicle, got dressed, gathered up all my things and left the hospital around 3.30pm. As I was due in for my operation the next morning I headed off to Sainsbury's in Cobham to do the big weekly shop to ensure we had everything we needed for the next week. And I treated myself to another magazine to take with me in the morning (there's always a positive!)

I finally got home around 5pm and Clive and Jackson asked how the day had gone and what had happened. I started to tell them about the day when both of them started to say loudly something along the lines of "We don't know what you mean, you're not explaining it clearly!" It was the final straw for me at the end of a fairly uncomfortable day. I got a bit upset so left them to it and headed off up to my bedroom where I had a few tears. It had been a pretty shitty day and tomorrow was not one I could honestly say I was looking forward to one bit. In one way I couldn't wait to get it over, in another I knew that things would be different for a while. I gave myself a positive talking to, changed the pictures I was running in my head and went back downstairs to make dinner.

> *When you change the pictures in your head (in your imagination) you can change how you feel. To feel a certain way we have to look at the film / picture in our head first. A lot of clients will tell me that they don't see anything they simply feel it. They haven't realised that they have looked* at a *picture however fleetingly to recall the feeling. To prove to them that they do need to look I ask them to recall a feeling without moving or de-focusing their eyes. It's amazing what happens.*

After dinner I packed a small bag with the items the hospital recommend I take with me – dressing gown, wash bag, my magazine and I put in my trusty bag of nuts, raisins and dates ready for when I came round. I knew I'd be offered a drink and either biscuits or a sandwich post op, neither of which food items I was eating. I checked that my iPod and iPhone were fully charged. I had a shower and washed my hair. I looked at my right breast in the mirror covered in crosses and laughed. It did look really funny. I dabbed it dry so as not to remove any of the crosses.

I went downstairs to watch TV and sat in my normal spot on the small two-seater sofa. We have two gorgeous long-haired cats called Bentley and Pepper. Bentley usually likes to sit on my lap, if Jackson isn't in the room. He jumped up on the seat next to me and went to climb on to my lap. He put his two front paws on my leg, stopped, gave me the strangest look, meowed and backed off. He stood looking at me from the other seat for a minute or two then again went to climb into my lap. Again he stopped and meowed loudly, looking at me. After a few seconds he backed off again and went and sat down on the other end of the sofa. He was looking at me as if to say, "Something ain't quite right with you tonight". I had drawn Clive's attention to watch Bentley's behaviour and how odd it was. I commented to Clive that perhaps he could sense the radioactivity in me and didn't like it. I tried picking him up but Bentley wasn't having any of it and moved back to his end of the sofa, where he sat looking at me for the rest of the evening. We went to bed early, as we had to be up around 6.15am to get to the hospital in the morning for 7.30.

CHAPTER 9

Admission Day

It was dark, cold and wet outside. I went into Jackson's room to say cheerio, have a good day and see you later. He gave me a sleepy hug, wished me luck but said that he knew I'd be fine.

The benefit of going to the hospital at that time in the morning is that you can park wherever you like. We parked in the end as close as we could to the SSSU (Surgical Short Stay Unit). We rang the bell. A nurse arrived, checked my name and details on the list and then she took us into a bay on the left with six beds in it. She took me to the last bed on the right next to the window – not that you could see anything out of the window as it looked on to nothing but a featureless wall.

Clive sat in the chair and I sat on the bed. The curtain was drawn between my bed and the bed next to me but was open at the end of my bed. I looked around the bay. There was a young girl in the first bed on the other side of the bay. Next to her was a lady with her leg in plaster who looked as if she had spent the night in the unit and was now waiting to be discharged. The bed opposite me was still empty. Eventually all the beds in the bay became occupied.

Clive and I chatted a bit – you know, the sort of small talk you make when visiting someone in hospital. I could see he was worried and I was determined to stay as upbeat and positive as possible. It was important that he see I was Okay with everything. In some ways I think it was much harder for him than it was for me. I'm so positive that, looking back, it really didn't allow him not to be.

After 8 o' clock it started to get busy with various doctors and anaesthetists coming and going. Eventually a young man appeared at the end of my bed and pulled the curtain around it. He was carrying a file – my notes – and he sat down on the bed next to me. He introduced himself as James and said that he would be my anaesthetist throughout my operation, he was very relaxed, smiled a lot and actually looked at me while he was talking. My previous experience of anaesthetists was that they tended to be cold, look at your notes while talking to you and then hurry away.

James was definitely like a breath of fresh air. He opened my notes and apologised for asking me the questions he knew I'd been asked a million times before but needed to check name, date of birth, address etc. Then came a list of questions about things like whether I had false teeth, metal plates anywhere or contact lenses. As he was talking a female appeared around the curtain and introduced herself as Lucy, one of Mr Kissin's registrars. She joined in as James started to explain what would happen through the day. At some point during the morning I would be taken down to X-ray and have a wire inserted to mark the tumour so they could locate it when operating. After that it would be a case of waiting on my bed. A nurse would then tell me when to get changed into the gown. I was third on the operating list so Lucy and James thought it would be around 11.30am when I would be wheeled down to theatre. James said he would be looking after me throughout the operation. He went on to explain that a blue dye would be injected into my breast which would highlight the lymph nodes and turn me slightly blue as my lymph system carried it around my body. The closer to the injection site the bluer it would be. Another Smurf image came to mind. The injection would take place once I was asleep and in theatre. They both explained that a very small incision would be made to remove the tumour along with the sentinel nodes but, as they weren't expecting them to show any signs of the cancer, that would be it.

James then asked me which breast I thought it was. I told him the right he asked to see it. Both he and Lucy commented on the number of nodes that were marked. James then drew some large arrows on and around my right breast. We laughed and joked about how anyone could possibly get it wrong now! My right boob looked like a road map with lines, arrows and crosses all over it. His good sense of humour was perfect for me and I felt very relaxed about the whole thing. When they finished marking me up they asked if I had any questions. I wanted to make sure that there would be "no surprises" when I woke up, they both knew what I was suggesting. Lucy said the worst case scenario for me would be that the sentinel nodes, when tested, turned out to be what is called OSNA positive.

OSNA stand for One Step Nucleic Acid Amplification – a test that now allows consultants to be told if there are any cancer cells present whilst the patient is still in theatre.

The benefits are that women no longer have to have the agonising two-week wait to find out the results and, if positive, the need to return to surgery for a second operation.

If the result of the OSNA test was positive then they would remove all the nodes they could find that had been marked up, which for me would be quite a few. I would know as soon as I woke up, as I would have a drain inserted under my arm. The drain is needed as the lymph nodes carry the fluid around the body.

Obviously with some of them removed it would have nowhere to go and would simply collect in that area. The drain is removed once the body has adjusted.

As they were explaining everything Clive became upset and couldn't help having a few tears. He had been trying so hard not to show his emotions, he kept saying he was sorry and expressed guilt that *he* was upset when *I* was the one going through this. Seeing Clive upset made me feel guilty that he had to watch this happening and that I was putting him through this pain and worry when I knew I was going to be fine no matter what. I wished that I had just got him to drop me off then texted him approximate timings to call the unit, that way he wouldn't have been subjected to all the detail (especially as watching any sort of operation on TV is not his idea of fun!).

James and Lucy were really good, checked that he was okay and asked if he had any questions. He asked a couple of things and they reassured him. James said that he thought I should be back in the unit by about 1.30pm so Clive should call in then. Due to confidentiality between patient and consultant Clive would only be told that I was okay and not given any details. Once they were sure the anaesthetic had worn off enough for me to go home then he could come and collect me.

PAUSE FOR THOUGHT...

I so wished I had known more about the impact of what I put into my body back in my twenties so maybe I could have done something about it. Let's be honest: at twenty years old I was working for Laker Airways as an "air hostess" (now they are called cabin crew) travelling the world and having fun. One-week Barbados trips, four-day trips to LA, Toronto, New York and, boy!– did I know how to party down route? As Clive says, my diet when he first met me consisted of vodka and chocolate! A bit of an exaggeration, I did eat other stuff as well but not

---

particularly healthy food. Sugar played a big role in my diet: I loved desserts and always wished I could start a menu backwards to make sure I had room for them. Whether I would have changed my habits back then, knowing all this about sugar and cancer, when you tend to think you're invincible and live for the moment is another question.

I made myself a promise that the positive outcome of all of this would be that I could at least now start to inform others, especially women, about what they are storing up, particularly in their twenties and thirties, for the future. I want them to think about what they are putting into their bodies and imagine sometime in the future what it would be like to have to tell their children they have cancer, diabetes or some other serious disease. We are having children later in life than in my parents' generation so the chances are that when they get to that risk age bracket their children will still be at school. Breast cancer in women is increasing at an alarming rate, in fact not just breast cancer but all cancers are increasing. I learnt the hard way that ignoring the knowledge we now have about what we put into our mouths and making believe "it won't happen to me" is pretty stupid. Look where I'd ended up!

We have no history of breast cancer in my family – well, we didn't but we do now. From now on my sisters and niece, and any granddaughters I may have in the future will always have to answer "Yes" to that question on forms: "Has anyone in your family had breast cancer?" My son will have to answer "Yes" if forms ask him, "Has anyone in your family had cancer?" and then of course he'll have to give details.

There was no point in looking back. All I could do was take control of what I do now, hence my change in diet and keeping my stress levels low!

James asked again if I had any further questions and was I absolutely clear what they were going to do. He then asked if there was anything he should know or that I wanted to tell him. I explained that in the past, including my recent operation in August, I had taken a bit more putting to sleep than normal and appear to be quite resistant to the effects of anaesthetic. He laughed and said, "Oh, so you're one of those patients that I need to get the elephant-size dose ready for!" We laughed and joked about it.

Having read in Love, Medicine and Miracles about the body's ability to respond to instructions under anaesthetic I also wanted to test it out if the need arose. So I explained to James a bit about what I do, and the relevant passage in the book, and said if they needed me to do anything, like reducing bleeding, to raise or lower my blood pressure or to make my lymph nodes more visible whilst under anaesthetic, simply to ask me. I'm not sure what he thought but at least I'd planted the seed, just in case!

I signed the relevant consent forms and they left, with James saying to me see you later and to Clive, "We'll take good care of her for you."

After they left Clive and I had a chat about it all. I wanted to reassure him as much as I could that I was fine and there were lots of positives to all this. I said he might as well go – I was okay and he couldn't do anything sitting there. I knew he had a busy day with guitar pupils and was pleased that he would be busy so as to keep his mind occupied during the time I was due to be operated on. I didn't need him thinking about it and giving the "pendulum excess potential". He agreed and said, as you would say in these situations, "If you're sure you're okay then I'll go." We hugged and kissed, he checked again that I was okay. I said I was fine and would see him later. With another hug he walked down the bay and gave me a final wave as he disappeared around the corner.

I had a knowing look and smile from the woman with her leg in plaster opposite and the lady directly opposite me. I realised that if I could clearly hear the conversations that had taken place behind drawn curtains then they had obviously been able to hear the conversation we'd had with James and Lucy and therefore knew why I was here. I took out my iPod and magazine and sat down in the chair. A little while later a young girl appeared at the end of my bed (funny how they all seem to be young – shows I must be getting old!). She checked my name and said she was from the X-ray department and would I follow her. I put my things away and followed her out of the bay. She told me to wait by the nurse's station with another lady. She then went off to a different bay and came back with a third lady following her. We all made small talk as we followed her through some large plastic swing doors out of the unit and down various corridors to the X-ray area.

She asked us all just to wait there until we were called. I looked at the clock. It's amazing how important the time seems to become when you've nowhere to go and someone else has control over your movements for the day. It was ten past nine. The three of us made a bit more small talk, then the conversation dried up as each of us went into our own thoughts. I remember one of the women

(I would guess around my age) picking up a gardening magazine and we had a chat about her interest in gardening. The other woman was a lot younger than us and this was apparently a second operation for her. She had been in before Christmas and needed a second operation as they hadn't removed sufficient tissue.

I was called through second to the X-ray room. There were two women in there, they checked all my details again and asked me to remove the top clothing and take a seat. Another lady appeared, introduced herself as a doctor and explained that she would be giving me an injection to numb the area and then using the ultrasound machine would locate the tumour and insert the wire. She checked my details again and which breast I thought it was. I made them laugh when I said that with all the markings I had on my boob I'd be amazed if they got it wrong. She made a couple more markings – my boob was starting to look like a map of Spaghetti Junction! I took my mind elsewhere again – my beach and sunbed in Barbados was getting well used and I was getting a lovely tan! She took a while to locate the tumour, having to push hard with the ultrasound equipment, and commented how small the tumour was. She thought it looked smaller than 7mms. That was the best thing she could have said. I wanted proof that what I had done mentally and physically worked and here I was on the verge of finding out. She explained about the wires they used and how they inserted them. She located the site and inserted the wire from the top of my breast pushing it in. Once she was happy it was in position she secured it with a piece of sticky tape and told me I could get dressed again.

I dressed carefully making sure I didn't disturb the wire, thanked them and left the room to take a seat outside again. The last woman was finally called through. When she reappeared we were all taken back to the unit and our various cubicles. As I returned to my cubicle I looked at the clock – it was now approaching 10.15. I got my iPod

74

and magazine out again and made myself comfortable on the bed.

I kept my eye on the time as it was getting close to 11.30 and as yet no one had told me to change. I continued to read and listen to my music. When I was still sitting on the bed at 11.40, I texted Clive to let him know that as yet I hadn't gone anywhere. I sent him another one at 11.50 saying, "Still here so don't ring until at least 2 o'clock". I thought that at least that way he wouldn't ring in at 1.30pm to find out I wasn't back yet and start to worry that something was wrong. From my own experience I know it is so much harder when you aren't there, have no idea what is going on and can't get any news – that negative voice can really get going and get you to imagine all number of dreadful things to be true!

Shortly after I'd sent that text a young woman (yet again another *young* girl – I've decided that the definition of old is when everyone seems younger than me!) appeared around my curtain with a gown and some compression socks. I got changed. I put my clothes in my bag in the cabinet at the side of the bed. I told her I was ready and she came back round the curtain.

She unplugged the electrics in the bed and tried to change the height on the bed but it wouldn't work. She explained that the beds had a battery but obviously it was flat on my bed and it would only work plugged in. She apologised and said she would need to check with theatre that they were happy that the bed would only work plugged in. She told me to take a seat in the chair again. Ever tried sitting down on a cold vinyl chair with one of those open-at-the-back hospital gowns on and no underwear? I decided to remain standing in my lovely compression socks. I looked down at myself and wondered if I could start a new fashion trend! She reappeared a few minutes later to say that they were happy. So I climbed onto the bed, she drew back the curtains and we were off. As we turned left out of the bay I saw the sign for the loo and thought (excuse the language – and pun) "Shit, I meant to go to the loo before heading for theatre. Oh well, I'll ask to go when we get there". We turned left again and through the big plastic double doors, down various corridors and we were soon into the theatre area.

You can tell it's the theatre area by the change in people's uniforms. Now they're wearing the loose fitting tunics and trousers in the telling blue and green, with what always looks to me like J-Cloth hats on their heads, and those hideous Croc-type shoes. That's just my personal opinion of that type of footwear.

She pushed me into a bay that will take three beds side by side. I asked if I can go to the loo and received the bad news that there isn't one in the theatre area but she offered me a bedpan. I declined at the thought of using one of those doesn't do a lot for one's dignity and I thought it might only be down to nerves. I could see a clock at the nurse's station. The time was now really important to me as I wanted to know exactly when I went to sleep and exactly what time I came to – silly I know but just one of those things I like to know. Just after 10 past 12 a tall man came to the end of my bed and explained that he assisted James, the anaesthetist. He went to the head of the bed and wheeled me out of the bay, along the corridor and into the ante-room (the room where they administer the anaesthetic with doors leading into the actual operating theatre). Right above the door leading into the theatre there's a clock – yippee! I could see precisely the time I went to sleep. There was a small gap in the door and I could just see the operating table, the large light above it and people moving around inside.

James was now of course in his theatre wear and greeted me with a big cheery smile. He had to check all my details again, and *again* checked which breast they were operating on. That question caused us all to laugh as I said that if it wasn't clear to everyone in theatre then I'll be worried as it meant they need glasses. As he was preparing everything he asked more about NLP and TFT. I told him that they would need to be careful what they said in theatre, my unconscious mind would be listening – and reminded him that if they needed my help to simply ask. I had found it fascinating when I had read about it in *Love, Medicine and Miracles* and it made perfect sense to me. I was so desperate to try it out! His assistant asked me to sit forward so he could place electrodes on my back (as obviously they would be in the way of the operation on the front) ready to connect me to the ECG machine. James wiped the back of my left hand with an antiseptic wipe and inserted the cannula, securing it with a bit of tape. He explained exactly what he was doing and that the cannula would be used to inject the anaesthetic, and also for any other drips needed. He picked up the syringe from the table on my right, walked round the bed and inserted it into the cannula. He kept me talking and I fixed my eyes on the clock. I could feel the anesthetic flow up my arm as it was cold. James was still getting me to talk and then I could feel that lovely feeling of everything starting to fade away from me. I told James, "I'm off to sleep now, see you later", took one last look at the clock (it was just after 12.15) and closed my eyes. I was vaguely aware of them talking for a few seconds more but it was as if they were way off in the distance. I couldn't be bothered to listen...

CHAPTER 10

Out of Theatre

The first thing I can remember is being vaguely aware of something in my mouth and throat, wanting to get it out but being unable to do anything about it. Next, I remember waking up in a large theatre recovery area with lots of other beds and patients. I immediately looked for a clock. I was on the end of the bay, to my left was the nurse's station and there above them was the clock. It was 10 to 3. Blimey, I'd been out for just over two and a half hours. I did a quick calculation in my head from the times James had given us – down to theatre around 11.30 – Clive could call in by 1.30, as I should be back in the unit. Hmm, so he had estimated two hours to be back in the unit and clearly over two and a half hours had passed and I was only just in recovery.

As I was working this out I wanted to sit up in bed and became aware at this point that I had a tube coming out from under my arm. I had a drain in. Immediately I registered that the longer theatre time and a drain meant that, contrary to what they had thought, my nodes must have been infected and therefore they had had to remove them. I wanted to investigate the site of my operation further.

As I looked around the recovery room I was aware that to my right was a nurse. She came over when she realised I was awake and introduced herself as Emma. I wanted to sit up so I lifted my right arm over my head to see if there was anyway I could pull up a pillow or the bed to be a bit more upright. She looked shocked and in a very surprised tone of voice said something like,

"Oh, you've moved your arm over your head!"

"Oh my God, am I not meant to?" I exclaimed, at the same time as quickly bringing my arm back down to my side.

"Yes, it's fine," she said laughing, "it's quite
I'm just surprised! It's very unusual for women
their arms much at all, let alone right over th
after the kind of operation that you've just had."

"Well, I never read the instruction leaflets telling me
about how I should feel post-op."

As we both laughed, she operated the controls on my
bed to raise the back so I could sit up, then gave them to
me along with a buzzer to push if I needed anything.

"Would you like any pain relief?" she asked.

"No thanks, I'm not in any pain at all, but would it be
possible to have a drink of water?"

"Yes, okay, but you should sip it very slowly."

When she left me I had a look down the neck of my
gown. Something hurt up on the bony area rather than the
fleshy part of my body above my right breast and slightly
to the right of the centre of my body. I wasn't expecting
something to hurt up there. A look underneath my gown
revealed some sticky plaster holding a dressing over what
was obviously an incision that had been stitched. I wasn't
sure why that was there. Further investigation revealed a
very, and I do mean *very*, blue right breast. Okay, I was
expecting blue but not quite *that* blue. Smurf boob!
Further round to my right I could feel another lot of sticky
tape and large dressing and a bit further on from that I
could feel the tube going out from under my arm. It pulled
my gown round from the back as it made its exit over the
side of the bed. I looked over the bed to follow the tube
and there was my drain hanging on the side of the bed. The
only way I can describe it is that it looked like the tube
was going into a plastic concertina and the other end of the
concertina lead to an upside-down surgical drip bag. The
concertina bit was collecting a watery red fluid –
obviously coming from me! The bag beneath it was
currently empty.

Once I'd established what my situation was physically,
I had a good look round. There were several beds to my
right, and more beds directly opposite them. Then there
79

was a gap in the wall and I could see more beds beyond, with large doors to the left of them.

I was wide-awake, hungry and could have got up, dressed and gone home. In contrast everyone else seemed to be drowsy, sleeping or being attended to as they came from theatre. Emma commented on how alert I seemed and not at all drowsy. I explained that I, like one of my sisters, seemed to be able to come round really quickly from operations and when we did it was if we'd never had any anaesthetic. I drank the glass of water she had brought. I then set about using some TFT to check and clear any Individual Energy Toxins I may have had during the op, the anaesthetic being one of them, and tapped for what is known in TFT as psychological reversals.

I had just finished treating myself with TFT when a man I'd never seen before came and stood to the right side of my bed to talk to me. He introduced himself as Ash. It turned out he was one of the registrars. He explained what they had done: they had removed the tumour and surrounding tissue as well as the sentinel nodes. Unfortunately one of the sentinel nodes *was* OSNA positive so they had taken more lymph nodes, hence the larger incision rather than the key-hole one, and a drain. As I had the drain I was to be admitted to the hospital and would not be going home today. He said he would see me later up on the ward, and left.

My heart sank. Oh no – a night in hospital, my worse nightmare. I'm one of those people who like it to be completely quiet and more importantly pitch black at night. I know lots of people find it difficult to get a good night's sleep in hospital because of the noise, but add in the light and I've got no chance, but there is always a solution to manage things.

Emma came back after Ash had left and asked if I had understood what he had said about my operation. I said yes, I had understood that it had been far more than they were expecting to do. I looked at the clock and it was now gone four. I asked Emma if she knew if Clive had called yet as I knew he would be worried about me. She said she was sorry, she didn't know, as he would be calling the unit where I had been admitted. She told me I was to be admitted to Elstead ward and they were waiting for a bed to become available. As soon as they had one I would be taken up there. I asked about my belongings and where they were. She said they would still be in the unit and when I was taken up to the ward they would be brought there. I wanted to go to the loo but thought I'd wait until I got on the ward and go there.

Emma asked if I was hungry, as normally patients would be given something to eat and drink when they got back to the unit or ward. As she wasn't sure when that was going to be, she could bring me something now. They had a small supply of biscuits or sandwiches in the recovery area. I thanked her but explained that since my diagnosis I wasn't eating sugar or wheat, amongst other things, so that discounted both the biscuits and sandwiches. She asked the reason why and I explained the rationale behind it. She became even more interested and we had a chat about diet and getting healthy and why I had started drinking more water a couple of weeks before the operation.

As time went on I was getting more concerned about Clive because I knew he would be really worried. He would have phoned, probably several times. He'd have been told not to come and pick me up as I was being admitted. I was aware that, due to patient confidentiality, he wouldn't have been given any details about the operation other than it had gone well and I was "comfortable".

I was also now desperate to go to the loo. I pushed the buzzer and Emma came.

"I need the loo," I told her, "I'm bursting, can I go?"

"Sorry, no," she said, "You mustn't get out of bed. You'll have to use a bedpan."

Yuck! She went away and brought back one of those grey-coloured ones made out of what looks like very thick card. I was glad to see she did remember also to bring me some tissues. I took one look at it.

"I reckon that's going to be way too small!" I said.

She just smiled as she drew the curtain round. "Can you manage, do you need any help? Okay? Buzz when you've finished."

Have you ever tried using a bedpan? I managed to get it in place but once I started peeing I couldn't stop! I was aware that my bum was now wet – which meant it was definitely *full*. I buzzed and Emma reappeared.

"I told you it wasn't big enough," I joked, but actually I was highly embarrassed and apologised profusely as I knew it was, shall we say, more than full.

Emma was great and just laughed. As she removed it she showed me how green my urine was due to the dye they had injected into my breast. So here I was with a blue boob and bright green urine. I could only laugh. She got rid of the bedpan and with the help of another nurse changed my bottom sheet – which of course was now stained bright green! As they were changing my sheet Emma asked if I wanted any pain relief yet as it would definitely have worn off from the operation. Again I said no, thank you, I really wasn't in any pain as I had been treating myself in my own way.

Emma explained to the other nurse that even with the size of my operation I'd had no pain relief whatsoever since coming out of theatre. She asked what I meant by "treating myself" as she had seen me doing something with my hands. The thought crossed my mind that this would be the point at which she thinks I've completely lost my marbles, or that the anesthetic hadn't worn off and I was hallucinating!

> *I told them I was using a technique called Thought Field Therapy and went on to explain how it works by tapping on certain acupressure points. I explained about psychological reversals and how to clear them, also Individual Energy Toxins. I showed them how I'd cleared the effects of the anaesthetic and how I was treating myself for pain. They finished changing my sheet and pulled the curtains back.*

It was now early evening and there had been lots of people who had come into the recovery area and been wheeled through the double doors at the end. I was still sitting there with not a lot to do other than to watch what was going on – and think about Clive. I kept an eye on the clock and was now very concerned about him and what he had been told. I knew he would be really worried and desperate to see me or at least talk to me.

I became very aware of a man, in the bed diagonally opposite me, regaining consciousness and being given a drink of water by the nurse looking after him. He kept looking at me and I smiled at him but wasn't sure if he was fully aware of what was happening. He did say to his nurse, after yet another look at me, in a voice that was a bit too loud, "That lady over there looks very, very poorly."

Luckily Emma heard him and came over to me and explained, "Don't look in a mirror for a while, you might have a bit of a shock. The dye they use not only turns your urine green but turns your skin an ashen grey colour. It makes you look very ill."

So here I was with a tube hanging out of my side, blue boob, green pee, looking like death and with a very fetching hospital gown on. Hmm... nice look! The image of myself made me laugh.

Emma kept checking on me, taking my pulse, temperature and blood pressure, and apologising that I was still there. We had further chats about what I did and the type of clients I helped. Other nurses were now chatting to me in between dealing with the coming and going of patients. I must admit, as a people watcher, it was fascinating to see everything that was going on and listen to the chat at the nurses' station. I was now very hungry and had drunk quite a bit of water but was determined I was not going to do the bed-pan thing again. I slowed down my drinking.

Just before seven thirty Emma and a porter came to my bed and started to wheel me out of the recovery area. Emma said it was good news as the ward now had space for me and I was off to Elstead. She was at the end of her shift and another nurse volunteered to take me up to the ward so she could go. Emma declined and said that she wanted to make sure was I okay and settled on the ward before she went home. On the way up to the ward Emma and I chatted some more about what I did.

As I arrived in the ward a nurse from the SSSU appeared with my bag of clothes and belongings that she placed on the end of my bed. Immediately on my right was the nurses' station and they swung my bed into the first bay on the left directly opposite. The bay had space for six beds. Five were already occupied and my bed was wheeled into the sixth space, the last one on the right hand side, next to the window. The curtain between my bed and the one next to me was drawn closed. Emma made sure I was comfortable, gave the nurse on the ward my notes, told me it was fascinating to talk to me and wished me well with my recovery. I thanked her for all her help and she left.

CHAPTER 11

On the Ward

As we entered the bay I had noticed the toilet (hurrah!) on the right hand side and I was definitely ready to use it. The nurse on the ward came to see me briefly, I said that I needed to go to the loo and went to get out of bed. She stopped me and said she would bring me a commode – mildly preferable to the dreaded bedpan. I felt a complete fraud causing more work for the nurse, as I was quite able to walk and really wanted to go and use the toilet.

The nurse came back in a short while to retrieve the commode and introduced herself as the night Staff Nurse. She looked at my notes. When she saw that I hadn't been given any pain relief since leaving the operating theatre she was horrified and said she'd get me some straight away. I stopped her and told her that I had been offered pain relief all through my time in the recovery room but that I hadn't needed any. I wasn't in any pain then and I wasn't now. She gave me a very disbelieving look and said, "Are you sure?" I reassured her that I was fine. I didn't enlighten her any further. She chatted to me for a while and said I was obviously fine to get up and walk about. She'd get a bag to put my drain in so I could carry it about easily when I wanted to go to the loo. *Go to the loo!* Music to my ears! I was happy in the knowledge that I could now drink loads more water without having to suffer the indignity of a commode or a less than generously-sized bedpan.

She reappeared with my material "flower bag", or my new fashion accessory as I called it. The upside-down-looking drip bag at the end of the drain was placed inside my fashion accessory and was hung back on the hook on the right side of my bed.

My next priority was to text Clive to let him know I was all right, was now on Elstead ward and that he could possibly come in and visit, although it was past visiting hours. Clive texted me back a few minutes later to say he had rung the ward to ask if he and Jackson could visit. A nurse explained that visiting hours were over and that two male visitors on a female ward was inappropriate. But then she had quietly and helpfully suggested that should I "need something" it would serve as a pretext so Clive (but not Jackson) could visit for a few minutes. So he asked me what did I "need". I replied that he could bring me some fruit, some more nuts and my phone/iPod charger. I had devoured the nuts and raisins that I had in my bag and was still hungry having missed dinner on the ward. He said he was on his way and looking forward to seeing me.

I texted my elder sister Jen, in New Zealand. It was nine in the morning for her. I said I had been admitted to Elstead ward at the Royal Surrey, I was okay and that Clive would call her later. She texted back straight away, wanting to know why I had been admitted. I told that I'd had some lymph nodes removed and therefore had a drain fitted, but I was fine. I put my phone down and looked out the window. I was overlooking the large hospital chimney, the grounds and apparently the helicopter landing pad. Beyond were the lights of Guildford and what I thought was possibly the A3 with distant cars going up and down.

As soon as Clive saw me I could see how relieved he was to see that I was alright. His face still showed some concern and he checked again that I really was okay. I remembered that I must look a funny colour so explained about the dye making me look like a zombie. I told him what the situation was and that I hoped to be out the next day. Well, that was my plan, as I could see no reason for staying in. The registrar had said he would come and see me again when they had finished operating.

It was good to see Clive and be able to reassure him that I was fine even though things hadn't gone quite to plan. I checked how Jackson was. He said Jax was a bit disappointed I wasn't going home and he couldn't come and see me, but he sent his love. I was fine now I had

86

something to eat, had my phone charger and had seen him. I said I would text him when I had spoken to the registrar and we could sort out how I was getting home.

Clive then had to go and said he'd keep his phone by him overnight in case I wanted anything. He knew I wouldn't sleep because it was far too light and noisy in the ward. I told him it would be like doing a night flight and I'd stick my iPod in, hence wanting the charger as I could see that I would be using it a lot, along with texting on my phone.

After he had gone the drug trolley came round and various drugs were dished out to each patient. When they came to my bed they again offered pain relief saying that I might need it. I again declined. In my world what is the point in filling your body with drugs if you don't need them? I had drunk all the water in my jug and asked if I could have some more. I was determined to wash out all the anaesthetic drugs and as much of the dye as possible, and to rehydrate myself.

The light and noise were really annoying so rather than get upset by it I decided to get my iPod out and select my night-time playlist. I had received a few texts from friends, which I replied to.

There are always things in life that you can't have control over, but you can control how you respond to them or how they make you feel. If I had focused on being annoyed it would have made things seem worse and made me even more frustrated and tense. Instead I looked to see how I could change my situation and therefore affect how I felt about it inside.

I was listening to my iPod and looking out the window when the registrar, who I'd seen earlier in theatre recovery, appeared at the end of my bed. He drew my curtains around the bed and picked up my notes from the end of my bed. He came and sat down on the bed. He announced himself again as Ash and I clarified that he was one of Mr Kissin's registrars.

"Do you remember what I said earlier?" he asked.

"Yes," I said, "but could you go through it all in a lot more detail for me?"

"Of course, but first I'd like to look at the site of the operation. I've seen your notes. You haven't had any pain relief, is that correct?"

"Yes," I said, "I haven't been in any pain. The only part that feels a bit sore is where the dressing is, up near my collarbone. I wasn't expecting to find a dressing there. It feels like I've been punched."

"Sorry about that," he apologised. "Actually that incision wasn't really necessary. They thought there was a lymph node there and had tried to locate it. They did quite a bit of pulling and pushing around the area but weren't able to find it. I'm afraid you'll have a scar there for no reason."

I reassured him, "From my viewpoint one extra little scar isn't a problem. I'm happy they checked." I did make him laugh when I asked if Friday was a BOGOF (Buy One Get One Free) day for scars in theatre!

Ash explained Mr Kissin had removed the tumour and sentinel nodes for testing and as they had not expected them to be infected he had stitched me up. When the result came they had to "unstitch" me, make a larger incision, remove all my nodes and then stitch me up again.

He said, "Mr Kissin actually performed your operation but I had to stitch you up twice." His tone made it sound like it was my fault he'd had to do it twice. Right at that moment there was something about him that I didn't warm to and I wasn't sure I liked his manner. For some reason my defence-attack mechanism was suddenly on alert to do verbal battle with him if necessary.

> *The tone of voice you use can have a huge impact on the way in which a message is received or the way in which people respond to you. You can say the same words in several different tones of voice and it will portray a different meaning. Take the words "Thank you" – they can be said with a genuine, sarcastic or angry tone – same words but the delivery can convey completely different meanings.*

I asked what the consequences of the nodes being infected meant going forward. He said it meant that chemotherapy would now be an option on the table for my follow up treatment. My immediate reaction in my head was, nope, I'm not having my body filled with poisonous drugs and I'll manage it a different way. However I didn't say this to Ash, as somehow I didn't think he'd be very understanding of the "weird" stuff I did.

So the only thing I could think of to say in that instant was, "No, I'm not having chemotherapy. I'm self-employed and can't lose my hair, I won't get any work."

Even as I said it I knew it sounded a pathetic excuse but that obstinate, pig-headed bit of me that says black, even though I know it's white, came to the fore.

He got slightly short with me in his tone. "Why on earth wouldn't you take every medical option available to you?" he asked, obviously irritated. "And anyway you could get your hair cut short well before the start of chemotherapy. "

Actually it really wasn't about my hair but about the effects of the chemo drugs, which I hadn't researched before my operation as I wasn't expecting it to be on the agenda for me. However his manner, tone of voice and unwillingness to listen to me, and what I was feeling had really caught me off-guard.

Ash went on to explain about the drain. It had been inserted to take away the fluid from under my arm that the lymph system would normally carry around my body until my body had readjusted. It was for this reason I had been admitted and would be in hospital until the amount of fluid collecting in the drain was down to 50ml of fluid over a twenty-four hour period. He anticipated that would be at least until Thursday. I had to get home for Jackson before his exam on Monday so he'd know I was all right and it wouldn't have a negative effect on his exams.

My immediate reaction was, "No, I'm going home tomorrow!"

"I don't think so. You'll be in here until much later in the week."

"I am going home tomorrow," I repeated.

He was quite brusque again: "I'll see you the morning," he snapped. "You don't seem to realise the size of the operation you've just undergone."

He replaced my notes at the end of the bed, turned and left.

By now I had drunk another jug of water and was in need of the loo. I climbed out of bed, unhooked my fashion accessory and walked to the washroom at the end of the bay. As I entered the washroom there was a mirror right in front of me and I was surprised at how grey-blue I actually looked. If I looked this colour seven-plus hours after the operation no wonder the man in recovery had thought I was ill! I couldn't resist investigating further and had a look at the dressings covering the wounds, the site of the drain and my very bright blue boob! My pee was still a lovely bluey-green colour. I chuckled to myself. As I went to move I felt a tug at my side from my drain. I had placed it on the floor and forgotten to pick it up!

> *I climbed back into bed and continued to do my TFT and reiki treatments, and work on a visualisation for my new drainage system that would include turning off the "taps" under my arm. I pondered on it for a while then thought that if my plumbing at home sprung a leak then I'd call in a plumber. So as I had done in the Jarvis Centre, I got the guys in. I imagined that I had a small team of plumbers working under my arm plugging the leaks and turning off my taps. Next I needed to work on re-routing my drainage system.*
>
> *I saw my lymph system like an Underground map and thought what would I do if a couple of Tube lines were out of use on the route I wanted to take? I'd re-route and use other lines that would get me to where I wanted to be. So I imagined my lymph system re-routing and joining up with other "lines" until it had a continuous path.*

I'd be lying if I said I didn't shed a few tears on my own in the middle of the night. I was now very tired, hungry, wondering what the implications would be of what they had discovered and I just wanted to be home. I thought about Ash's comments with regards to my hair. Even now that it was going grey and had highlights in, it was still earning me compliments (which I must say is down to my amazing hairdresser, the lovely Des). I thought about what it would be like to lose it if I *had* to have chemotherapy. I decided if I were to wear a wig I would have some fun and have one that was nothing like my real colour. I pondered on it for a while and decided I'd like a long red one like Bree Van De Kamp in *Desperate Housewives*. It would then be obvious that I was wearing a wig and I could explain to people what my situation was without any awkwardness on their behalf. Once I'd embraced the idea of my red wig the thought of losing my hair was much easier to come to terms with… however I still wasn't sure I'd agree to have chemotherapy.

I continued to drink lots of water and take regular walks, with my fashion accessory, to refill my jug and use the loo. I set myself a little challenge of having clear urine by the morning. I can't resist a challenge.

My sister Jen rang the ward and they brought me the phone. She was surprised when I spoke to her as she hadn't realised they would bring me the phone. She wanted to know all the details and was all for me staying in hospital until they wanted to discharge me. I explained to her about Jackson and she thought that I should stay another night if that's what the hospital recommended.

After I got off the phone to Jen I decided to go and have a wash before breakfast came round. I looked in the mirror, still a tinge of blue showing on my face. I ran some water and took off my gown. I could now clearly see the extent of the dressings and steri-stitches.

As I wrung out my flannel and went to wash under my arms I was suddenly aware of the numbness along the underside of my right arm. It was really peculiar: here I was washing up and down my arm and I couldn't feel a thing! I literally had to look at what I was washing to make sure I'd washed it. It was a little disconcerting. I prodded around my arm, up and down it to work out the extent of the numbness. It went about two-thirds around my arm and all the way from my armpit down to my elbow. I dug my nail in to test just how numb it was: couldn't feel a thing. I finished washing as best I could and put the gown back on again. I gathered up my things, went to move away from the sink and tripped over the drain, which pulled sharply in my side. Yep, I'd forgotten to pick it up from the floor again. This was going to get annoying!

I was really hungry and looking forward to having something to eat. Imagine my disappointment when all that was on offer was a range of cereals and bread-type products. I looked for a boiled egg, piece of fruit or something of that nature. Nothing. Disappointed, but I guess I wasn't really that surprised. It emphasised to me the lack of nutritional knowledge around food in hospitals. I had two choices: eat nothing or choose something from the menu. I knew I needed to eat so had a tiny portion of cereal with a really small amount of milk. I chose a mug of hot water. I had a piece of fruit and some nuts left from the things Clive had brought in, and ate those. When my tray was collected the lady left a menu for lunch from which I could choose several items. There was a selection of sandwiches and hot food. I chose, as best I could, food that was not wheat, not covered in a sauce (dairy) and not containing sugar. Needless to say the options were very limited!

The day staff came round, first to take our temperature and blood pressure, then with the drugs trolley. Again they asked if I would like some pain relief. My lack of pain relief was now becoming a bit of a joke with them as they were saying things like, "Can't we even tempt you to a paracetamol?" It was so interesting to see how unused they were to patients refusing drugs.

The doctor's round had started. I saw a group of people gathered at the nurse's station. One of them was Ash, so I guessed it would soon be my turn for a visit. A young doctor came to the end of my bed and took my notes, saying they would be back to see me in a short while. I watched him like a hawk. He went back to the nurses' station, gave my notes to Ash who opened them, looked towards me, spoke to the nurses then to the young doctor who nodded in agreement – he was definitely junior. After a further discussion and some more nodding of heads Ash and the junior doctor came to speak to me. Ash drew the curtain around me, glanced at my notes again and said quite abruptly, "Good morning. You want to go home today? Fine, you can go."

I started to reply, "If you really think it's better for me to stay another night…"

But before I could finish the sentence he said, "No, you either go today or stay until your drain is taken out later in the week. We don't do discharges on a Sunday and I see you haven't had any pain relief."

I could feel a lump in my throat and tears starting to well up. I hadn't meant to be difficult, I just wanted him to listen or at least enquire about my reasons for wanting to go home.

He didn't bother to ask but I explained to him anyway that I wanted to go home because my son was due to take a Math's A level exam on Monday and his future at university depended on his grades. I wanted to make sure he had nothing to worry about and could see I was fine.

At this point Ash softened very slightly in his manner and said, "There are times when being a Mum takes priority and this is obviously one of them. You can go as soon as you have your discharge papers."

Now it felt like I was leaving one of the armed forces. He said the nurse would explain about my drain and there would be a daily phone call from the hospital. When the collection of fluid was reduced enough over a twenty-four hour period then I could pop back and have the drain removed. With that he pulled back the curtain. The junior doctor gave me the sort of smile that said "Sorry…I think he was a bit abrupt and I empathise with you", turned and followed Ash out of the bay.

Emily, the lovely Staff Nurse on the day shift, came up to me soon after Ash left to confirm I was being discharged.

"I don't think Ash was too happy with me," I said to her. "I reckon he thought I was being difficult."

"Ignore him," she said, that I was obviously bright enough to be able to follow instructions with regards to the drain, had had no lasting effects from the operation and hadn't taken any drugs. She lifted the drain up onto the bed and explained what I needed to do each day. A doctor would ring me each morning to find out how much had collected over the twenty-four hour period. When the amount was down to around fifty millilitres then I would be able to have the drain removed. I was also to keep the wounds as dry as possible. The steri-stitches would fall off by themselves and I was not to force them. She went to get me some large waterproof dressings that I could use to cover the wound. Once I had a bag of those all I needed was the discharge letter then I was free to go. I texted Clive, Jackson and everyone who had been in contact to say I was coming home and should be ready by the afternoon. Jackson texted back to say he was pleased I was coming home. With neither Clive nor Jackson available, I got Clive to ask Helen to come and pick me up. If she hadn't heard from me before visiting to say I was ready, then to come in at visiting time and hopefully I'd be ready to go by then.

Lunch came and went. Visiting time started and Helen appeared, it was good to see her and we sat chatting about all that had happened. Emily kept coming up to apologise that I was still there but they were still waiting for the letter. She had bleeped the doctors to request it but when they are on call discharge letters are the last things to be attended to. She said I could get dressed as literally all we needed was the letter.

Visitors came and went, the afternoon tea lady came round, dinner was served (Helen and I shared it) and we were still sitting there waiting. I could now understand why I had been held in theatre recovery for so long waiting for a bed. Clive had texted to say he was now home and where was I? I explained what had happened. He said if he'd known he would have come to the hospital as he had driven right by it on his way home from the gig.

Emily was brilliant. She kept us informed and apologised constantly. It was now 7.30pm and I had been waiting for the letter since Ash left me at 10.30 that morning. Emily came over again and said this was getting ridiculous. As I wasn't being sent home with any drugs she said she would ask the Ward Sister if I could go and they would post the discharge letter to me. A few minutes later she came back with the news that I could go and they would post the letter. She apologised profusely for keeping me all that time and now here I was going without it anyway. I didn't care, I was just glad to be going home. She emptied my drain one more time before I went.

Helen collected up my bag of things for me. I picked up my fashion accessory and hid it under my coat, holding it with my left hand. We were ready to get out of there. Emily told me that if I had any worries or concerns I was to call the ward immediately, not to even think about it for a second but to call, day or night, they were still there to support me. I thanked her for all her help and we left.

CHAPTER 12

Home Sweet Home!

I was so pleased when we pulled up in the drive. It was so good to be home, it felt like I had been gone for a week rather than thirty-six hours. So much had changed in that time and things were not as I had expected. I had my drain, which I certainly hadn't bargained on, and two larger scars than I had anticipated. I settled down on the sofa and Bentley immediately got up from where he was sleeping and climbed gingerly into my lap, sniffing around my wound. He meowed as if to say he knew something wasn't quite right but then purred, settled down and went to sleep. I was fine and in fact felt a bit of a fraud just sitting doing not a lot.

It wasn't long before Jackson walked through the door from work. I think he was as pleased to see me as I was to see him. He gave me a big hug and asked about the operation and what was in the bag. I explained what it was; he was intrigued as to how it worked (not really surprising as he wants to be an engineer). When he had finished asking questions he said, "I'm glad you're home, Mum," with a look that I knew meant he was relieved to see me. In that moment I knew that my slight disagreement with Ash had been worthwhile. I ate my dinner, enjoyed every mouthful of it, then drank my lovely cup of tea. Home!

I headed upstairs to get into my pyjamas. Managing the drain in PJs was so much more comfortable than the gown at the hospital. The only problem was I kept putting the bag down and then would walk away to get something only to feel the tug in my side. This was going to be a real pain (although not in the physical sense) when I wanted to do something. When I finally climbed into bed I continued to do my reiki, TFT and visualisations that now involved turning the taps off and building a new drainage system. I also envisaged the wounds healing quickly.

Sunday I woke up early and had some breakfast – it was so good to have my own food again. Around nine-thirty the phone rang. It was one of the doctors from the hospital. She introduced herself as Vicky and asked for the measurement from the drain. I read the total to her and then did what I had been shown in hospital. Vicky said she would call about the same time each morning to get the reading.

I spent a very lazy day in my PJs and dressing gown, sitting on the sofa watching *Ally McBeal* and intermittently doing my own treatments and visualisations. I still had a very blue boob, my pee was now a pale green-blue, but now in addition I was passing what I can only describe as green cowpat-coloured poo!

By Monday morning I'd had enough of just sitting around. I got washed and noticed some of the steri-stitches were coming away from the wounds as I changed the dressing. It did look funny to have this tube coming out of a little hole in my side and yet not be able to feel anything. I had thought it was coming out of the same wound as where they had operated but no, it had a little hole all of its own just behind the main incision. The main wound was obviously red and raised but I could already see what a neat job Mr Kissin had done and that in time it would be a lot less conspicuous.

I got dressed and headed into my office to answer emails and do some work. A long-standing client rang asking if it was possible to have an appointment with me. I explained that I'd had a small operation and had a drain in. If she didn't mind seeing me in my office at home, fine, I could keep the drain more or less hidden. She was happy with this and we arranged an appointment for the next morning, much to the horror of Clive.

I was starting to get used to my fashion accessory although occasionally, like when cooking dinner, I'd go to move a short distance and forget to pick it up. Ironing (believe it or not, a job I enjoy!) was much easier. I could put my bag on the floor and do the whole lot without much movement. And to think they wanted to keep me in hospital all this time!

> *If you set your mind to do something it's amazing what you can achieve. I was listening to my body and running my recovery according to how I really felt, not how others had told me I would / should feel.*

Vicky rang each morning as promised, and I was glad to be able to report that the amount which was draining out was getting less and less. By Wednesday the drain had slowed up considerably and was down to the desired amount for having it removed. Vicky said to go back to the hospital on Thursday afternoon and she would remove it. This was just as well as I had a full afternoon of clients booked in to see me at the clinic on the Friday.

I couldn't wait for Thursday afternoon and to be separated from my fashion accessory once and for all. The bag was quite full and getting heavy when hanging on my arm as I moved around. Vicky met us in the day ward. She was a young House Officer. She took us through to an empty bay with six beds in it and told me to undress to my waist so she could get to the drain. She went off to get a trolley with the necessary equipment to remove the drain. She removed the dressing covering the drain and my wound and had a good look at the wound, removing the final few steri-stitches that were still attached. Next she cut the tube between my side and the pump, to release the vacuum that was necessary to drain the fluid out of my body, and took away my lovely fashion accessory. I wasn't sorry to see it go. Finally she came to remove the tube from my side, which she said was held in with a stitch that she would need to cut to pull the tube out.

As she was looking at the site where the tube entered my body she said, "You seem to have healed exceptionally quickly and have actually got skin covering the stitch and tube." She explained that the only way she could get the tube out was to remove the stitch and the only way she could do that was to cut the skin that was now covering it. She apologised.

"Don't apologise," I said, "it's not your fault. Go ahead."

Eventually she managed to get it and pulled the tube from my side. Interestingly I could feel it being pulled out; it felt funny but not painful. Finally she put a small covering over the cut she had made and checked both my scars. The smaller scar (my buy-one-get-one-free scar!) had healed and lost all the steri-stitches a couple of days after the operation and was now just raised and red. The larger scar had also healed beautifully but was also, as you'd expect, slightly red and raised. She again commented on how fast my draining fluid seemed to have reduced and how well I had healed in a few days. I briefly explained what I had been doing. It felt great to be able to get dressed without a tube sticking out of my clothes!

I thanked her for her help and we left the hospital. Freedom at last from my unwanted accoutrement! That evening when I got ready for bed I started rubbing Rescue Remedy cream over the scars as well as all over my right breast in addition to tapping the area to clear it of any reversals.

Now the next hurdle was the outpatient's appointment with Mr Kissin, a few days before my birthday, on Wednesday 26th January at 4.10pm, for my results. We would then know what my next stage of treatment was going to be.

I believe that the universe gives you what you need so I wasn't too busy with clients through January. I had enough work to keep "the wolf from the door". I also noticed that as the day went on my right breast seemed to harden and swell slightly, and I became aware of the "golf ball" sensation under my arm. There was still a blue tinge left from the dye and the area of numbness in my arm was greatly reduced, about half the size it was, and I now had more areas of tingling. I had full movement of my right arm but when reaching up over my head could feel something pulling down my side and it was slightly tender on the muscle going from the scar around to my back.

CHAPTER 13

The Follow-Up

The three weeks from the operation to the outpatient appointment seemed to be more intense than the time from my diagnosis to the operation. As far as I was concerned I was now being treated and what came next would be all part of the healing process. There was a reason that my lymph nodes had been infected and although it wasn't obvious then I was sure it would become clear at some point in the future. However I was convinced that things would be fine because of everything I had done to help myself. I had simply excluded my lymph nodes from my visualisations due to the information Mr Kissin, in good faith, had originally given me.

I knew that radiotherapy was going to be on the cards for me regardless of any other treatment. Some years ago I had read research that said aloe vera was good for protecting against the effects of radiotherapy. I had purchased it for several friends in the past who were going through radiotherapy and their skin appeared to have had very few of the common side effects. I went to our great little health shop in Hersham and bought some organic aloe vera to drink as well as a bottle of organic aloe vera to rub over my right breast. I believed that by starting to rub a good moisturiser in now it would build up a great protective layer – as you might do a week or so before going on a summer holiday to protect the skin from sunburn.

Thursday 26th January arrived, exactly two months since I had received the news at the Jarvis Centre that I had breast cancer. I joked with Clive that both our birthdays were now going to be very significant. Clive decided that he wanted to come to this appointment with me and hear my results. As we headed for the hospital car park. I could sense that he was feeling very anxious about my appointment and results.

When we arrived in the outpatients' area for Mr Kissin's clinic and took a seat, Fia, my breast care nurse, spotted me and came over to have a quick chat. I introduced her to Clive and she said she would come in when I was called through to Mr Kissin. We didn't have to wait for long before Mr Kissin came out of a consulting room and called my name. We went in, sat down and Fia sat behind us on the bed. Mr Kissin disappeared into the next room and came back with my file. He looked through but couldn't find the results he wanted. Fia searched through as well. He was saying to her that he had told the clinic that he needed all the results and they had said they were all here for him. He told Fia to go and find all the results. She disappeared out of the room. Mr Kissin apologised to us and asked if we would mind waiting outside again. We got up and went back out into the main waiting area and sat down. By now Clive and I had gone quiet. I could feel how anxious he was.

No sooner had we sat down than Mr Kissin reappeared and said he had found some of the results and only my blood results were missing. He ushered us back into the room and asked another nurse to go and find Fia and tell her he only needed the blood results. We went back into the room and sat down again in front of the desk. Clive was sitting to my left. Mr Kissin explained that he would wait for Fia before he started and with that disappeared through the door into the adjoining room again.

Clive reached over and took my hand. I could feel my heart thumping while a million different thoughts were running through my head. This was worse than being in the Jarvis Centre on my own waiting to hear that I had breast cancer. Fia came in behind us and went through to the room next door with what must have been my blood results. A few seconds later she reappeared with Mr Kissin. He sat down at the desk and Fia sat down on the bed behind us again. He opened up my file and started

103

looking through all the various papers. He started by recapping on what he had explained to me in my original appointment. I wanted to say "Yes, yes, but what now?" However I resisted as he continued to go through it all.

"When the original biopsy was done in November," he said, looking over his glasses perched on the end of his nose, "the tumour was a grade two cancer. Somehow, Mrs Harvey-Bush, you've managed to downgrade it and when it was removed in the operation it had become a grade one cancer."

I knew it! I raised my arms from the elbow and pulled my fists back down with a whoop of "Yes!"

"It had also shrunk slightly from 7 millimetres to just under 6 millimetres," he added.

Double fist pump and another loud *"Yes!"* from me. It may not sound much but a reduction of approximately 15% in six weeks sounded good to me! As I whooped he peered at me over his glasses, perched as usual on the end of his nose, with a twinkle in his eye. He went on to say that he had performed the operation and it had been a little bit more complicated than he was expecting because I had a lot of muscle in that area.

"Muscle?" I asked, "as in, because I work out in the gym?" Ever hopeful!

"No," he replied, "You are very unusual in that you have an additional little muscle that comes from under your arm and up over your chest area. We had to cut it, release it and move it before we could do the operation." Clive and I knew that this had to be genetic because my nephew had discovered he also had an extra muscle on his right side.

It was interesting when I told people about my muscle discovery as they asked if I had one on the other side as well. I wouldn't have known about the one on my right side if it hadn't been for breast cancer and I have no intention of finding out if I have one on the other side!

Mr Kissin continued to describe the operation in some detail. "You are obviously aware that we had to take some of your nodes. We took five of the sentinel nodes out for OSNA testing and were surprised when one had come back as OSNA positive." He never mentioned that I had been stitched up then had to be "unpicked" again.

"Five nodes doesn't seem to be a lot," I commented.

He looked over his glasses at me again and continued, "We then removed twenty-seven level two nodes, so in total we took thirty-two nodes."

"Is that about average?"

"No," he said, "that's more than most, a lot of nodes". They were all sent for analysis and it turned out that only one of the sentinel nodes had microscopic evidence of any cancer cells."

I asked what he meant by "microscopic". He replied that there had literally only been two or three cells affected.

He looked back through my notes and various results. I could more or less feel Fia behind me itching to shout, *"Just tell her!"*

It seemed like an age before he looked up and said, "We've discussed it as a team, that includes the oncologist, and because it was only in one sentinel node, and the cancer had somehow been downgraded **and** the tumour had shrunk, we've decided that chemotherapy would not be part of your ongoing treatment. It will only be intensive radiotherapy and for you to continue taking Tamoxifen for the next five years."

Another big whoop of delight from me. Thank you universe, you sent me a message about my life, loud and clear, and I will heed it!

I could feel Clive give a huge sigh of relief. "Could I ask exactly what you mean about the downgrading?" he asked.

Mr Kissin explained something about the cells now turning over much more slowly than previously… but I wasn't really aware of what was being said as I was mentally dancing and whooping.

I thought I should tell Mr Kissin that I had stopped taking Tamoxifen after a couple of days due to the warning in the contraindications listed about someone close who had suffered a stroke.

"Who is it that has suffered a stroke?" he asked.

"My Mum," I said, "She died from one."

He then asked, as always looking over his glasses, "And how old was Mum when she died?"

"Seventy-three."

He gave me one of what I call his exasperated looks and sighs, and said firmly, "You are *hardly* like a wrinkled old prune" - I took that as a compliment - "so when you are a lot older we'll think about changing you to another medication. Until then just keep taking it."

That was me well and truly told.

Mr Kissin then asked me to undress my top half and sit on the edge of the bed so he could check the area. He asked me to move my arms this way and that and to raise them up as far as I could. No problem there! He was pleased with the way it was healing and told me I could get dressed. He then explained that the next thing would be an appointment with Dr Neal, the oncologist, to sort out my radiotherapy treatment and that he, Mr Kissin, would see me back in clinic in six months' time. He asked if I had any further questions. I was desperate to know if I could start exercising in the gym and doing my yoga again. He said that there was no reason why I couldn't start going to the gym but to avoid running for a few weeks. (He didn't specify what *he* meant by a few weeks and I didn't want him to clarify!) He warned me to remember that I no longer had the lymph system to deal with the extra sweat generated. So when I started exercising I needed to take longer over warming up to give my drainage system time to cope. He explained it was like having a bath that had no overflow to deal with sudden filling. In the same way I needed to avoid things like steam rooms, saunas and jacuzzis as they create sudden heat in the body. Hmmm, I wasn't too happy about that but thought I'd get to work on

106

visualising the building of some new plumbing. He went on to say that the plus side was that I wouldn't suffer from perspiration under my arm. So: reconnect my drainage system so I can have saunas or don't reconnect to avoid underarm perspiration. To sweat or not to sweat? That was the question.

"Any further questions?" he said finally.

"No, I don't think so, but this is the best birthday present ever. Thank you."

He replied, with a smile and a twinkle in his eye, "The cavalry arrived just in time. You've done your bit for cancer now, so you can go away and forget about it."

As I was busy whooping with joy I looked at Clive who was shedding tears of relief. He started to apologise for the tears and say he was happy but it was such a relief. Fia was very kind and reassured him. I think it was more difficult for those closest to me to go through it than it was for me. Fia moved us from the consulting room into another side room. She explained more about the removal of my lymph nodes and about lymphedema. She said that I needed to be aware of it and gave me yet another leaflet for my collection. Fia explained that I would now need to take Tamoxifen for the next five years but that I would be exempt from prescription charges. She told me what would happen next and to expect an appointment with Dr Neal, the oncologist, in the next few days. We thanked her and left.

By the end of the third week, post-operation, I was able to sleep more comfortably on my side or on my back without my breast "pulling" but I still didn't feel comfortable enough to sleep on my front. My breast was still tinged with blue but the wounds had healed really well.

As I now knew what the results were and what was to happen next we started to tell a few more people. There was now no need for people to do what I call the broken-neck "how are you?" question, when they tip their head to one side, nor any reason to avoid talking to me about it. The "pendulum" had stopped swinging.

CHAPTER 14

Preparing for Radiotherapy

I continued to see clients and work on the Virgin Flying Without Fear courses up and down the country. I was straight back into the gym as soon as I could get there. I admit that when walking briskly on the treadmill I could feel the impact on my right breast, it felt very strange and a bit uncomfortable. Several people commented that they hadn't seen me for a while and how good I looked with the weight I had loss. They asked what I'd been doing. I simply explained that I'd been diagnosed and treated for breast cancer. As a result I had, amongst other things, changed my diet and the weight loss, though not a primary aim, was one of the positive outcomes. They wanted to know exactly what I had changed in my diet and why. Where did I buy things like quinoa? What did the "raw food" recipes involve? Could I write the recipes down for them? And it was at this time that people kept saying I should write a book.

I received my appointment letter to see Dr Neal, the oncologist, on Tuesday 8th February at 3.30pm. Clive wanted to come with me to hear what was going to happen next and what the treatment would entail.

We found the clinic area that we needed to be in and sat waiting to be called through. Finally we were called through into a small consulting room and Dr Neal came in.

He went through my notes and reiterated what Mr Kissin had said about how they had come to decide on just giving me radiotherapy. He explained what the next stage of my treatment would be: six weeks of radiotherapy. For the first five weeks the treatment would be every other day, so three treatments in one week followed by two the next. However when I got to week six my treatment would change to daily and the area where the tumour had been would be specifically targeted rather than the whole breast being treated. They would also be using a different type of ray. Dr Neal asked to examine me, he also expressed surprise at how well it had healed. He went on to explain that I would be given an appointment to come in for a CT scan where I would be marked up with two small tattoos. These would then be used to line up the laser beams on the machine every time I came in for a treatment. My actual treatment would start approximately two weeks after that but I would be given a treatment plan with all my appointment times listed.

He asked if I had a preference for the time of day that I was treated as they would do all they could to ensure that my treatment was around the same time each day. I decided that I'd like a first thing in the morning appointment. That way I knew the treatment would be over and I would be free for the rest of the day work-wise.

Dr Neal asked if we had any questions. I asked how long each treatment took. He said that it would take longer to line me up each time than it would for me to have the treatment. The treatment itself would last for a couple of minutes. I thanked him and he left the room. We gathered up our things and the nurse showed us out. She told us that I would receive a letter in the next couple of days detailing my appointment for the CT scan and that it could be any time of the day.

On the way home I started to think about what I could do to help the process and protect myself from any side effects. Again I had chosen not to read the information leaflets so that I wasn't anticipating how I should feel or what I should or should not be doing. I thought about how my visualisation would need to change and pondered on what would work for me.

I continued to moisturise with aloe vera and drink it daily in preparation for the radiotherapy. I had decided that when I was having the actual treatment I would need some Jedi knights with their light-sabers in my breast. The sabers would absorb the "positive" rays that I needed, making them even more powerful, and they would obliterate the "negative" rays.

My letter arrived with my CT scan and tattoo markings appointment. Me! Getting tattoos! It made me smile. I had agreed with Clive that I would go for my appointments on my own, as it was pointless him driving backwards and forwards with me.

I still had some blue dye showing on my breast but I was sure they would be used to this! My arm wasn't feeling quite so "prickly" and the feeling was slowly returning to the area. The sensation of having a golf ball under my arm was also lessening; it seemed to be harder in the evening but was definitely feeling better.

As I was waiting for my appointment some ladies were coming in with headgear on, various wigs, hats and scarves and some proudly coming in with their "hair-free" heads on show. I admired every one of them but it really brought home, sitting there looking at them all, how common cancer was and that it didn't matter who you were or what you did.

I was called through and told to change into the robe and there were also plastic bags that were hanging up. I popped my coat back on over the top and went back out to the waiting area. I was soon called through to the scanner. I was told to put my things down on the chair and to climb onto the bed in front of the scanner. The two radiographers told me not to move or try to help them, as they would move me around as they needed to. They were using some laser lights to line me up and kept moving me a tiny bit this way, then a tiny bit that, to get me in the right place. Yet again pen marks were made all over my boob – this was becoming a habit!

I was aware that a man had walked into the small control room overlooking the room I was in, but I had no idea who he was at that point. Later he came into the scanner room and introduced himself as a consultant. I took my mind off to another place while they measured and drew all over me. When they were satisfied with the measurements the consultant double-checked everything and then left the room saying he would be back shortly. One of the radiographers went and got a trolley with some needles on and other bits and told me that she would now be giving me two tiny black dots as tattoos. She had some ink and a needle and did something under my arm; it felt like a small nick in my skin. The second tattoo was on my midline between my breasts, and that one I definitely felt because of the lack of flesh there. She dabbed them with cotton wool to absorb the excess ink and tiny drops of blood.

They explained that I needed to be measured up for the intensive week's radiotherapy I would be having in week six. My breast would be covered with something resembling cling-film and lined up with the tattoos and various markings to ensure they had the right position. We had to wait for the consultant to return to do that. They waited a while before attempting to bleep him but had no joy in contacting him. It was now getting close to five o' clock so they said he must have got caught up with another patient and that they could continue on another date when I was in for a treatment. I was told to go and get dressed and go home. They explained that my first appointment for a treatment would be in two weeks to allow them time to explain to the team what my treatment plan was. I would have a slightly longer appointment for my first one, so a radiographer could explain things to me and then I would have my first treatment.

I was still keeping to my new diet (and I use diet in the nutritional sense, not in the losing weight sense) to keep myself in tiptop condition for the radiotherapy. The fact the weight was still coming off, though, which was a real bonus. When I had weighed myself the previous week I was sixty-nine and a half kilos, so had lost eight and a half kilos (nearly nineteen pounds) and I knew I was even lighter now.

I received my appointment for my first treatment; it was to be on Monday 7th March at 8.40 in the morning. On Friday 4th March I was eight weeks post-operation. I still had a tinge of blue on my breast. I had full movement of my arm and didn't feel like I had a golf ball under my arm, even at the end of the day. The only time I was really aware that something was different was if I had been using my arm a lot, like carrying my laptop in and around London, then it "prickled" more and my breast appeared to harden slightly. Even though I was post-op I was still keeping to the diet whilst I went through my radiotherapy to ensure my "cells sparkled" and I had no unnecessary inflammation in my body.

I had now been drinking the organic aloe vera juice for two weeks as well as rubbing the moisturising version all over my breast in preparation for my radiotherapy. As my first radiotherapy session was on Monday I had started to increase the amount of water I drank to ensure I was fully hydrated. I had been rubbing Rescue Remedy cream over the scars to help them heal and they were fine, not pulling or annoying in any way.

CHAPTER 15

Me and My Jedi Knights

My new patient appointment was at 8.40am with the radiographer who would explain everything to me and give me my treatment plan for the six weeks. My first treatment was then booked in to follow the appointment at 9.00. I had been told I should be finished by 9.15.

I had some breakfast, filled a 750ml bottle with water and headed for Guildford. I parked, walked into the unit and checked in with the receptionist who sent me off down to the end of the wide corridor behind her, to area LA5 and told me to take a seat there.

Eventually a radiographer came out, called my name and said we'd go for a chat first. We went to the end of the waiting area and sat behind the screen where there were several chairs. She sat opposite me and checked all my details against her sheet. She handed me a sheet of paper with all my appointment times for the whole of my treatment plan. Most of the appointments were around 8.30 in the morning unless I had to see someone else on the same day, then they were at various times. It worked out that I was due to have five treatments over each fortnight, which meant that I would be treated Monday, Wednesday and Friday one week and then the next week it would be Tuesday and Thursday. At the end of the third week I had an appointment for a review with a senior radiographer as well as my treatment. There was one appointment on my sheet where I wasn't being treated and had to go back to the CT scanning unit. As I hadn't been marked up by the consultant (he had left the room and never came back) for my week six radiotherapy when I originally came in and had my tattoos, I needed to have that done. Finally in week six of the treatment plan I had daily appointments for the five days.

She went on to explain that as soon as I arrived each time to go into the changing room where I would find a pile of clean gowns and some plastic hospital bags hanging up. I needed to remove the clothes on my top half, pop them into one of the plastic bags, put the gown on with the opening at the front and, if I wished, put my coat back on to keep warm. When I was ready I was to come out and take a seat until I was called. When I had finished my treatment I should leave the empty plastic bag on one of the hooks in the changing room and drop the gown into the laundry bag on my way out. She handed me a leaflet on what to expect – which of course I didn't read – and asked if I had any questions. I didn't have any, so we got up and left the little screened area. She told me to go and get changed and then take a seat again until I was called.

Eventually my name was called. I followed the radiographer into where the machine was and she introduced me to a second radiographer. She told me to put my things down on the chair, to remove my right arm and breast from the gown and to lie down on the sheet on the bed. Bed isn't exactly the right word; it was more like a hard slab! Whilst I was doing that they checked my details, name, address and date of birth.

I lay down. They fixed in a handle slightly above my head and to the right, and asked me to put my arm back to hold on to it with my right hand. They then explained that they had to get me "lined up" using my tattoos and laser beams in the room. It would involve moving me small amounts on the bed until I was in the exact position required. It was better if I let them do it rather than attempting to help or move myself unless asked. One of the radiographers picked up a remote control at the bottom of the bed; the lights in the room were dimmed so that the green laser beams could be clearly seen. The bed was raised and moved into the correct position and they pulled the sheet a tiny bit this way and that, with me on it, until they were happy. At the same time one was calling out measurements whilst the other was checking and confirming or moving me a fraction until they were happy. When they agreed that I was in the correct position the laser beams were switched off and the lights in the room brightened again. They told me they would be leaving the room whilst the machine was working, but would be monitoring me from the other room. They asked me not to move until they came back in.

Whilst they were lining me up I lay back and started my visualisation, getting my Jedi knights and their lightsabers at the ready in my right breast. They would absorb the good energy they needed and bat back any energy that was harmful to me. I added in the whirring noise that the lightsabers make and made the picture big, bright and bold – they were ready for action.

The machine was up to my left and I lay waiting for it to start, not really sure what I was expecting to happen. I then heard a click and realised that it had now been turned on and boy, were my Jedi knights busy zapping their lightsabers this way and that! I counted in my head at the same time and I got to thirty before I heard the second click as the machine turned off.

Then the machine made some changes, shrinking down what I can only describe as its window area (I'm sure there is some technical name for it but have no idea what it is). There was a second click and off we went again for another count of thirty. Those lightsabers were shining bright by the end, full of positive energy. I saw the negative energy being hit right out of my body and dissipating into the atmosphere.

I lay perfectly still until one of the radiographers came back into the room and said, "That's it, you can let go now and move". She lowered the bed with the remote control and I hopped off.

I put my arm back into the gown and covered myself up again, picked up my bag of things and followed her out of the room. I thanked her and she said, "We'll see you again on Wednesday. You'll probably feel tired and need to rest. After a couple more treatments you'll start turning pink and be a bit sore as if you've been sunburnt." Up went my guard and those subliminal suggestions simply bounced off: being tired was *not* part of my plan, I had a business meeting to attend in London. As for turning pink and becoming sore, that wasn't part of my plan either.

I headed back into the changing room and tested myself for the radiation being an IET (Individual Energy Toxin). It was. I needed to clear it using TFT's seven-second treatment, so I checked if it was to be done on inhale or exhale. It was exhale, so whilst breathing out I gently pressed on the front and back of my head for three exhales.

I got dressed, left the plastic bag hanging up, picked up my bag and the gown and headed out of LA5, dropping the gown into the laundry bag on my way. From waiting to be called through for the treatment to leaving the unit it had been about fifteen minutes.

I returned to the car. The car park was now full and people were waiting to park, so getting an early appointment time was definitely worth it. Before I left I had a big drink of water from the 750ml bottle I had brought. My target was to have drunk all of it by the time I got home, my belief being that I was rehydrating from the drying rays of the machine.

Every morning and evening I continued to slap aloe vera all over my breast as well as drinking the juice before breakfast. I was still keeping to my nutritional plan, testing literally everything that I was using or consuming for IETs, tapping my reversals, as well as at night using visualisation and doing some self-reiki before I went to sleep.

Wednesday morning soon arrived and I was filling my water bottle, checking I had change and my parking permit with me as I headed out the door. Same routine as on Monday, two short bursts of treatment then free to go. My Jedi Knights knew exactly what to do this time.

By the time my Friday appointment was due I knew the routine well, from getting up in the morning to getting back after my treatment. I was also getting used to seeing the same few women at the hospital at the same sort of time as me. At the end of my Friday appointment the radiographer said that I would feel tired over the weekend and would need to rest. They really would make good hypnotists – "You are feeling tired, you are feeling very tired and have no energy". As usual I ignored the comment. I was off to the gym and then yoga in the evening. She reminded me as I left that my next appointment would be Tuesday as I only had two treatments the second week. Week one of radiotherapy completed, three treatments done and so far I was still feeling completely normal and full of energy. Bring on week two!

I still had a tinge of blue showing on my breast but it was very faint now, and I hadn't felt the "golf ball" under my arm at all during the week. I still had some numbness in the underside of my upper arm but I could now feel when someone touched me on my arm. I still couldn't feel the more subtle touches My breast around the operation site now felt much softer rather than hard to the touch.

I was very much the lucky one and had nothing to complain about. A few scars and some discomfort was nothing in the scheme of my whole life.

> *What I needed was another visualisation to boost the repair of the nerve endings. I imagined them returning to normal size and the communication between them being repaired – as you would with broken wires - so that they could fire from one to another easily all the way up my arm, my side and breast right into my brain.*

I went to the gym and managed to run one kilometer for the first time since my operation (I used to run between three and five kilometers just to warm up). My breast felt fine, a bit strange while running but I could only describe it as different. I had also decided to start yoga classes and went for the first time that evening. The only people who knew that I'd had breast cancer were Ali and Sara. As the teacher, Sara needed to know why I couldn't do certain moves yet.

I had a very busy week work wise during week two of my treatments with business meetings in London, a full day's corporate training to deliver as well as private clients to see. On Saturday I was due to deliver a talk at the BTFTA (British Thought Field Therapy) conference near Heathrow, then had to rush home, pack and be ready to head off to Southampton for the Virgin Flying Without Fear course on the Sunday. Still no-one was really aware that I was undergoing radiotherapy following my operation, or even that I had had an operation.

Week three of radiotherapy meant three treatments again, Monday, Wednesday and Friday. Treatment number eight on the Friday was also connected to a three-week review. My appointment sheet showed my treatment was booked for 1.35pm and my review for 2.20. By the end of week three the receptionists knew you by name as soon as you walked in and smiled as they marked you as in. My sheet indicated that my treatment wasn't in the usual LA5 area, as the machine was being serviced, but in LA2. Instead of having to walk all down the corridor and round the corner I walked a short distance to LA2. The same routine applied. Except this time instead of heading out the door I had to take a seat back in waiting area for the senior radiographer to come and get me. I saw a lady come out and look in the waiting area. She glanced at me then went back into her room, and so I went back to reading my magazine. She came out again and looked around so I looked right at her. She looked at me, then came over and asked if I was Gillian Harvey-Bush. Apparently she had looked at the photo in my file and decided it didn't look like me but I appeared to be the only female waiting in that area. We went into her consulting room and she explained that this was a mid-way check to ensure that I was okay and coping with the treatment. Had I noticed any side effects and how I was coping so far? I told her: no side effects and feeling fine. The only difference was that my right breast was slightly swollen compared to the left, but then it had been like that since the operation.

"How tired are you getting?" she asked.

"Not at all tired."

"How sore are you?"

"Not at all sore."

"How pink have you gone already?"

"I haven't gone pink, I'm still the same colour."

She started to look at me in a very disbelieving way, then said, "You need to be aware that the tiredness could kick in a bit later in the treatment, even a few weeks after it's finished."

Another subliminal suggestion I batted away.

I do appreciate that the medical profession have to give you as much information as possible, and most people want to know everything, but it is important to be aware of how those suggestions can impact on you.

> *I was not being flippant in my behaviour towards all the information and help but I was doing* **what I believed to be true and worked for me.**

She asked if she could take a look. She agreed that I had no sign of any pinkness or soreness, which they would expect to have happened by now. She said that it would go pink at some point as if it had been sunburnt, and my breast would end up a slightly darker colour than the other one. As I got dressed again she explained that weeks four and five of my treatment would be a continuation of the "proton ray" treatments, which were treating the whole breast. When it came to week six the daily treatments would be "electron ray" treatments, targeted specifically at the area where the tumour had been. Electrons were less invasive than protons.

She asked if I had any questions. I didn't. Finally she said, "You're now on the last part of your treatment. You're doing incredibly well."

By the end of the week the skin on my breast was feeling a little drier than normal so I was slapping on the aloe vera gel whenever I could and still drinking the juice daily as well. My arm was still a little bit "prickly", more so directly after the treatment, but eased when I did some tapping. In the interest of my own research I tapped some days and not others: the days when I didn't do my tapping the prickly feeling stayed all day.

Friday 1st April – April Fool's day. Week four of treatment completed. I only had two treatments this week but had to go today to get marked up for my week six treatments.

When I checked in at reception they asked me to take a seat in the main waiting area. There were a few other people waiting, including a woman and her husband. Fia, my breast care nurse, appeared and went to talk to them. I could hear her reassuring the lady and her husband about radiotherapy. My name was called and I was taken through to the CT scanning area that I had come to when I was originally marked with my tattoos. I knew the routine and went into the changing room to put on the now very familiar gown. I put my denim jacket back on top, went back out into the waiting area and picked up a magazine. Fia then appeared, accompanied by the lady and her husband, suddenly recognised me and laughed about my new fashion look of hospital gown and denim jacket. She asked if I was there to be marked up for my radiotherapy and when was it due to start? I laughed and told her that I was about to start week five of my treatment and was here to be marked up for week six. She was amazed at how good I looked and asked if I was experiencing any side effects. I told her that I was fine and had been to the gym and to yoga and so on. She laughed again and said, "But of course you would, with your allergy to negativity."

The woman who was with Fia had gone off to change. Fia then quietly asked if I would have a chat with her about my experience of radiotherapy. I was happy to talk to her and her husband. When she came out of the changing room Fia introduced me to her and it was clear she was very apprehensive. Fia explained who I was, at what point I was at in my radiotherapy and all the things I was doing, like the gym and yoga. She then left and the couple asked me all sorts of questions about the radiotherapy, what I had done and my treatment. The more I explained the more questions they asked: Why had I changed my diet? Why hadn't I read the leaflets? How was I able to do yoga? etc, etc. Then I was called through to have my marking done.

It was the same routine: take my arm out of the gown, lie on the scanner bed, hold on to the handle behind my head and let the radiographers move me. The difference was this time they lay a piece of clear polythene over my right breast (it felt like I was being covered in cling film). Various measurements were called out and, as far as I could see, markings were made on the polythene with pinprick holes. The door then opened and in came the consultant that I had seen the first time I had been marked. He apologised that I had had to come back as he hadn't been able to get back to me. I laughed and said that I had passed him in the corridor leaving with a lady on my way out last time but I realised it was Friday afternoon and he wanted to get home. He laughed as well and apologised again. He checked everything over and the markings that had been made. Before I knew it they were done and the polythene was folded up and put into my file.

I went back to the changing room, got dressed, came out and continued my conversation with the couple about my experiences. She was visibly brightening up right in front of me and said she had wished that she'd known all this before she had started her treatment. She had been through a round of chemotherapy and was dreading the fatigue everyone kept telling her she would get from radiotherapy. We had a lovely chat and she asked if she could have my phone number for a chat at some point. I was happy to give it to her. She was then called through. Her husband thanked me and said I had done so much to change how she was feeling and had given her hope and a very different way of looking at things. I told him he was welcome and I was happy to help in any way I could. I wished them both well and left the unit.

I felt enormously energised by the chat and it made me even more determined to help people who would like some control during their treatments, operations and visits to hospital. It wasn't a case of either conventional treatment or complementary methods, there is a third option: a combination of both. My mind started racing with ideas, as it often does. I knew then that this was another reason for having had my cancer – so I could use my skills to help others.

> *There are always positives in everything. Sometimes you're not aware why something that appears to be negative is happening to you, but weeks, months, even years later, when I look back in my life, I can invariably see a positive for something that appeared negative at the time. I was sure this was going to lead me to all sorts of other things I hadn't even dreamed of yet.*

Monday 4th April was week five and the last week of three proton treatments. I was really pleased with myself that here I was in week five and I had not really suffered any pinkness or soreness. My arm was still a little bit "prickly" and my breast felt – how can I describe it? – solid to the touch and tight at the top under my arm. When I moved my arm back it was like there was a muscle that was too tight, pulling at it. I was also starting to experience some hot flushes from taking the Tamoxifen, but only when I had forgotten to clear the toxins and tap my reversals.

It was a fairly normal week of work and zipping up and down the A3 with my big bottle of water. By now I had seen most of the shift rotations of the radiographers and got to know them a bit. Some were much friendlier than others. There was a particularly nice male from New Zealand. I hadn't seen him for the first few weeks and it turns out he had been home on holiday and had been staying a street away from where my sister lives! He had passed her house everyday as he headed for the beach. I had seen him and a female on the Monday but had a different couple of radiographers on the Wednesday, again one male (whom I didn't particularly like) and one of the quieter female radiographers.

The male appeared to be more senior. He was very offhand and asked what I had been using to moisturise my skin. I told him organic aloe vera. He told me I had to stop using it and switch to an aqueous cream. I questioned the reason, as I had no problems or dryness from the aloe vera. He said that it wouldn't be good enough for the following week of daily treatments. I was about to leave so I didn't question it any further, just thinking, "Okay, they obviously have a lot more experience of these things than me." I decided to do what he advised.

Was that ever a mistake!

I was busy working for the rest of that day and had an appointment in London early next morning so didn't get chance to buy any cream until I got home from London. I went into Weybridge and bought some E45 cream that he had recommended. I forgot to use it Thursday night but put some on, instead of my aloe vera, on the Friday morning. I went for the final treatment of my whole breast. Yippee! I couldn't wait to put a tick against it on my appointments sheet. I had got my visualisation off to a fine art by now and could even anticipate to the second the moment when the machine would switch off.

I had a busy day preparing for a small Thought Field Therapy course I was running at home on Saturday and Sunday. I went to the last yoga class before the Easter holidays and as usual had a good laugh. I came home, rubbed in the E45 cream and went to bed.

I was up early to make sure everything was in place for the delegates arriving for my course. I was aware by about lunchtime that my breast was starting to itch. Towards the end of Saturday it was really uncomfortable. I thought that it would stop if I rubbed more cream in. When the delegates had gone I went upstairs, stripped off and slapped on a load of E45. By Sunday the itching was driving me mad but I couldn't scratch as I was training! I was desperate, by the middle of the afternoon, to go upstairs, strip off and have a good scratch.

When all the delegates finally went and I'd packed up I headed straight for the en suite. I took my bra off and several layers of skin came with it. It was as if there was a

125

mould made of my skin inside the right cup of my bra. The whole area where I had been applying cream was now peeling, red raw and weeping constantly. My right breast was extremely swollen. I guessed that I had had an allergic reaction to the E45. I could have kicked myself. I had been so careful to check every little thing that had come near me to see if it was an Individual Energy Toxin but had forgotten to check the cream. I tested myself and sure enough it was a toxin for me. I put a loose top on but it was weeping so much that it wasn't long before the top was wet. I had to keep putting tissues gently all over my breast to absorb the moisture. It was late and I knew I was at the hospital early in the morning so thought it must stop weeping at some point soon. I would get it checked in the morning.

We went to bed; it was a really bad night for me. I lay there with nothing on top of me and a box of tissues next to me. My boob was itching terribly, but I couldn't – daren't – scratch it. It was very sore and it wept all night. I spent the whole night gently laying tissues over it, removing them when they were soaked and then repeating the process.

It was the first time I had felt really low since being diagnosed but kept thinking, "This is better than it was five minutes ago and in five minutes it will be better than it is now." I lay visualising it healing and drying up. I kept using reiki on myself through the night.

Monday 11th April was our 19th wedding anniversary – what a way to start it! I got up early and padded lots of tissues over my breast, taking the box in the car in case it leaked through my clothes. When I changed at the hospital I replaced the tissues with some new ones, then took a seat waiting to be called. It was the nice New Zealand male who called me through. "How have you been?" he asked brightly.

"I've had a bit of a problem," I told him.

When I took my arm out of the gown and he could see my breast he was horrified. "What have you been doing?" he asked. "What have you changed? You'd been doing so well, with no soreness, no redness, no problems at all."

I told him what had happened the previous week and the conversation that had taken place about aloe vera versus E45. Interestingly, the other female radiographer who'd been there when I was told to switch was in attendance this time too. She stood back a little sheepishly and didn't say very much.

"I'm very sorry, you've been given some duff information," said the Kiwi candidly. "You can't get any better that one hundred percent pure organic aloe vera. You've obviously had a really bad reaction to the cream. I'd like you to be seen immediately after this treatment in the clinic upstairs, but right now we still need to carry on with your programme."

I lay back on the bed with my arm over my head as per usual, except this time they retrieved the marked polythene from my notes and had to lay it on my red, swollen, weeping breast, lining it up with the tattoo marks. He was very gentle and kept apologising. The positive was that at least the cling film stayed put! With the size my breast was now I'd have given Jordan (aka Katie Price) a run for her money. The only difference would have been that *mine* was completely natural!

The machine was set up differently this time with a cone-shaped attachment added to it. It reminded me of an old concertina-type camera. He explained this was so they could focus the beam precisely at the spot where the tumour had been. The beam would also be made up of electrons, less invasive, more superficial than the proton treatments I had been receiving in the last five weeks. When they had lined everything up and left the room the machine was operated only once but my Jedi knights were ready. I knew that room so well and every sound the machine made.

When the treatment was over my friendly radiographer said that unfortunately the soreness would get a lot worse before it got better and my breast wouldn't recover until after all my treatment had finished.

I laughed and said, "No, I don't think so. That's your view, not mine."

He smiled, told me to get dressed again and take a seat whilst they sorted out a clinic appointment for me. I covered my breast in yet more fresh tissues, got dressed and settled down to read a magazine.

Eventually one of the radiographers appeared carrying my notes and took me upstairs to where the clinic was being held. She told me to take a seat and my name would be called but it might be a while, as they had to fit me in. Finally I heard my name called and followed a nurse into a little room. She asked me to remove my clothing from my top half and sit on the bed. The window was open and the room was cold, I sat shivering on the bed but with one burning hot boob. When she came back with the registrar they were both horrified at the state it was in. He asked what had happened, so I told my story again and he agreed that I had been given incorrect information and would have been fine on the aloe vera for the last week. He gave me a prescription for some Piriton, which would alleviate the itching, and something called Instillagel, which would numb the area slightly, disinfect it and help it to recover. He explained that the Instillagel would come in syringes and I was to use each syringe fully for one treatment twice a day. He left and I got dressed, padding myself with yet more tissues, and went to the pharmacy window. It was now well past eleven and I was pleased I had taken the day off, following the weekend of training, and didn't have any clients booked in.

Walking back to the car I was angry that I had been given bad information when I had been doing brilliantly. I was even angrier with myself for not testing for a toxin. I climbed in the car, took a large swig of water and headed for home.

I took a Piriton as soon as I got home. Clive wanted to know what had happened and what I had to do. I told him it was partly my fault for not having taken responsibility for testing it. There was no way we would be going out, even for a coffee, to celebrate our anniversary! I went upstairs to the en-suite and stripped off, carefully peeling the tissues off my right breast. I opened up the Instillagel and got one of the syringes ready to squeeze out the clear gel. It definitely felt cool, in an anaesthetic way. I lay on the bed waiting for it to absorb into my skin before getting dressed again. I did some reiki, tapped for my reversals and visualised calling upon those plumbers, who had helped after my op, to stop this leaking. When I'd finished I got dressed again, minus my bra as I had been advised, and continued with my day.

By Monday evening it was so much better. There was still a small amount of weeping but not much. My T-shirt only stuck slightly as I removed it ready for another dose of Instillagel. The itching had stopped altogether, which was a huge relief. Having had no sleep at all the night before, I went to bed early and had a much better night. I still did my tapping, visualisations and reiki before I dropped off to sleep. There was a lot of work going on inside my breast.

When I woke up on Tuesday morning there was only a small amount of me stuck to my top and all the weeping had stopped. I was able to remove the dry skin from the area across my chest that wasn't being subjected to radiotherapy and once again apply my normal, lovely aloe vera.

My appointment for my treatment was at 1.35pm, to be followed by an appointment in Dr Neal's clinic at 2.30. I had a client to see in the morning so plenty to keep me occupied. Luckily when I arrived at the car park it was around lunchtime so I only had to wait a short while to get a parking space. I was now definitely counting down the treatments: only four to go including this one. I checked in at reception and headed for LA5. I was now so used to the routine: into the changing room, bag your clothes, take a seat and wait to be called. The same radiographers were on duty as had seen me the day before. They were really surprised when they saw how well and different my breast looked compared to twenty-four hours earlier. They both said they couldn't believe it was so much better – they would have expected it to be a lot worse. My breast was still slightly swollen but so much better than Monday night – and of course not as good as it was going to be in a few minutes and it would be even better a few minutes after that!

I had my treatment, got dressed and went upstairs to wait for my appointment with Dr Neal. He read my notes and asked how I had been. How was I coping with the tiredness and side effects? I explained I'd not been at all tired and in fact had been working throughout as well as going to the gym. He asked to see my breast (this was beginning to be a pattern – come to the hospital and strip off!) He apologised for the incorrect information I had been given, particularly as I had been doing so well. Apart from that episode he was pleased with my treatment. Three to go, then I would be discharged from radiotherapy. There would be a follow-up appointment with Mr Kissin in July.

When I woke up on Wednesday the whole area had improved enormously. There were some dry patches of skin still on my breast that needed to come off (I felt like a creature shedding its skin!). The outer edges above the breast and on the other one had actually already returned to my normal colour.

This morning I had two of the other radiographers. One was a nice young girl who I had been seeing throughout so was now very familiar with. The other one was the "quiet" lady who had been with the male radiographer when he told me to change to E45. They both agreed I was looking okay. The young one asked what had happened, as I had not shown any adverse effects previously. I told the story again and the other lady (my "witness"!) apologised for not speaking up and for not saying that I didn't have to change creams if I didn't want to. She hadn't foreseen a problem so had thought it unnecessary to contradict her colleague. She said that she had learnt a lesson, so next time she would speak out to prevent this happening to anyone else. So here I was, as a result of my negative experience, hopefully helping people again, albeit indirectly.

Finally when I treated my breast with the Instillagel that evening I noticed that the blue tinge had gone and there were no traces of blue dye beneath the red. Whoop! Whoop! Smurf no more. I had a very slight, intermittent stabbing pain in my breast but nothing I couldn't ignore. I was nearly there! Two more treatments to go then I could concentrate on getting my boob back to normal.

My final treatment came on the Friday morning. When the treatment was finished the young radiographer I had seen a lot came in and explained the information on my discharge form, gave me some "just in case" information and told me an appointment would be sent for me to see Mr Kissin. I thanked them for their help and said not to take this the wrong way but I wasn't planning to see them again under these circumstances.

I left the room for a final time, got dressed, dropped my gown into the laundry bag for a final time and walked off down the corridor aware that I had a grin on my face from ear to ear and a real spring in my step. Hooray! It was over, finished, *finito! DONE!* I climbed into the car, took a great big swig of water, took out my appointment sheet, put a final tick next to the appointment and wrote "Yippee!!" below it. I had been given cancer for a reason, it was telling me something and I had listened. Life would now be very different for me.

CHAPTER 16

Reflections and Observations

Friday 29th April and two weeks had passed since my last radiotherapy treatment. The dry, flaky skin had improved dramatically. There was still a small patch of dry-ish skin in the circle area where the booster treatment had been targeted but over the last few days even that was now settling. The swelling had all gone and my breasts both looked the same size. The radiotherapy had given my right boob a slight "tanned" look with a slightly darker line underneath it, but nothing too obvious. I still had a loss of sensitivity in the under part of my arm and on my breast where the tumour had been.

I was now concentrating my visualisations on getting the sensitivity back into all areas. The next date in the diary is 27th July when I have to return to Mr Kissin's clinic. I'm assuming I will now be "downgraded" to seeing one of his registrars rather than him, which is fine with me.

Reflecting back over the last five months and how I've dealt with it, from picking up the letter and just "knowing" what the diagnosis was to now, I can honestly say I never worried about it. I have had my moments of realising, acknowledging that I am different both physically and emotionally. I've got some scars, a couple of tattoos that look like big blackheads, I'm minus some lymph nodes and I'm not sure what will become "normal" for me in the long term. It has also raised a lot of questions for me about how I live, deal with things, and what emotions I need to express or share. In the past my tendency has been not to say anything when I've been upset or annoyed in order to avoid conflict or upsetting those close to me. It seemed so much easier all round just to keep my thoughts to myself. Then I discovered I had to live with the consequences. Looking back over the years there were many things that I've felt unable to share with anyone and have simply kept to myself. It seems quite appropriate now so say that maybe I should have got them *off my chest.*

I have a theory that I've come to whilst going through this process and from reading Dr Siegel's book. As a coach I found it fascinating listening to other women who were going through the treatment at the same time as me, or have been through it, talking about their lives and the language they used to describe it. Working on the basis that people are holding an emotion somewhere in their body, because of the *dis*-ease in their lives, it's interesting when you look at where they get their cancer.

When I'm coaching, my clients often give me a fair idea about how they are feeling emotionally, and often physically, by the language they use: "I'll be okay when I break the back of this work" – "I feel like I'm shouldering total responsibility" – "I just can't get my head around what's happened" – "My life's crap at the moment" – gives me a clue as to what has perhaps been going on in their life. I wonder, once people with cancer can identify, express, acknowledge and deal with the emotion they have been holding on to, if that would allow the body to heal fully.

For example, kidney cancer. What do the kidneys do? Simply put, the kidneys filter the waste out of our blood and balance the volume of fluids and minerals in the body. Therefore perhaps the person with kidney cancer needs to clear out the waste or rubbish from their life that they may have been hanging on to for years and get their life back into balance again. Lung cancer: the lungs are crucial for breathing – so perhaps that person has felt suffocated in some way or area of their life. The medical profession can treat the resulting physical symptoms but if the root cause isn't addressed does it prevent the body healing fully? Will the same result happen again in a few years time if the *dis*-ease they have in their lives isn't changed? I **emphasise** it's just a theory. I'd need to research it further by meeting up with others to identify what they might have been holding on to inside that manifested in their particular cancer.

I definitely felt there was a change in me, but how and what I should do now, moving forward, wasn't completely clear to me. My feelings were different as a result of reflecting on all I'd just been through. The type of work I do was definitely going to change. I wanted to inspire others so that they too could take control of their lives in so many ways not just when diagnosed with an illness.

I had had an interesting experience while talking to a friend about my cancer and how I had dealt with it. During the conversation her friend who was with her said, "It's all very well going through it all positive and happy but won't you feel silly when it comes back?" My friend looked shocked and a bit embarrassed. I could almost literally feel my brain processing what she had just said.

*Not IF but… "**When it comes back**". ??!!*
*There was an automatic assumption on her behalf and I realised it said an awful lot more about her than it did about me, about the way I approached life. I replied that I could have adopted a "woe is me" attitude, being really grumpy and unhappy about what life had dealt me. Alternatively I could go through it being positive and happy, with a good outcome as I had done. **If** it should return I would approach it in the same way, as I preferred being happy than being miserable and feeling sorry for myself. She looked a bit disgruntled and didn't say much more, but I could see she was running her own version of **how I should be** in her head. It made me realise just how much I had changed over the years and how much happier I was being **this** me.*

My breast was now looking much more normal and the numbness in my arm had nearly gone. I had experienced some "cording" in my arm from below my breast, up my side and all the way down my arm to my wrist. I understood why they call it cording; it really did feel as if there was a bit of cord inside me that was too short and needed stretching out – a very bizarre sensation! I visualised a long piece of cord stretching and flexing like elastic as I stretched my arm out in front of me and raised it above my head. Within a day it had gone.

I had been warned that post-op I would only perspire under my left arm, and this indeed had been the case. I took it as a positive – only one sweaty armpit to worry about. But on a particularly hot day just before we went on holiday I noticed that I was perspiring under both arms. It looked like my plumbers had been busy rebuilding me a new drainage system. That was a *real* positive.

My follow up appointment soon came round. As predicted I saw one of Mr Kissin's registrars. She checked me over and said everything was fine and that I had obviously healed very well. I asked about the tightness I was feeling when stretching my arms backwards and she confirmed that it would be internal scar tissue pulling. The next appointment would be for a mammogram in January, a year on from my operation, and then another appointment to be seen in the clinic the following August. The clinic would follow me for five years (which is how long I had to take Tamoxifen) and I would have yearly mammograms for ten years. I thanked her and left the clinic.

How did I feel seven months on from the op? I felt great, the seven months had gone really quickly, eight months since diagnosis. I was chuffed with myself for how I'd approached it and gone through it. I was so pleased I had taken an **active** role in my care and not just simply handed myself over to the medical profession for them to resolve it. I was pleased I hadn't read any leaflets or jumped on the Internet to bring up even more subliminal suggestions. I had gone through my *own* experience, listened to my *own* body and not experienced what others said I should. Whilst I had been sitting in outpatients waiting to be called I had overheard two different women talking to breast care nurses. Both had been through an operation (one had had a lumpectomy but no lymph nodes removed) and radiotherapy. They were questioned about their energy levels and fatigue during and post-radiotherapy. Both women replied that the radiotherapy had knocked them for six, they had felt exhausted and tired – just as they had been told they would! It was fascinating to listen to the various conversations and hear repeated again and again variations of *"I felt just as you said I would"*.

Life could go on as normal now. I was still keeping to my diet at least 95% of the time and my weight seemed to have stablised. The numbness in my arm had gone and the scars hardly noticeable. Mr Kissin had been just the right consultant for me and had done an amazing job with his team.

Just before Christmas I had received my anniversary mammogram appointment for January 19th at 11.30am at the Royal Surrey Hospital. Before I knew it the appointment day arrived.

A year on and how was I feeling? I tended not to think about it anymore other than when something specific reminded me. So thinking about it my breast was now practically normal. I'm glad that through the year I'd written down how it has felt, to remind myself that it is still improving.

The day of the appointment arrived. My right breast was to be X-rayed first. I leant in as it was being positioned ready for squashing. It was duly squashed in the vice-like grip of the machine. The instruction came to hold my breath (I already was!) while she operated the machine. Once the X-ray was taken my breast was released from the "vice" ready to be repeated from another angle.

The radiographer looked at my scar and commented, "Neat job. Was it Mr Kissin?"

"Yes, it was," I replied with a smile.

"You can always tell his handiwork. You were lucky to have him."

Finally I got dressed and she told me I would get a letter in the post with the results in the next two weeks. If I hadn't received it in two weeks I was to contact the radiology department. I thanked her and left.

Next target: clinic appointment in August. Life was good.

My final observations, as I finish writing this book about my personal encounter with cancer, concern about how people react to it. As I was going through my treatment I met lots of women all dealing with it as best they could with the knowledge they had. Family and friends supporting them in the only way they knew how. Fortunately my years of self-development had equipped me with tools that not many other women seem to have. The money I had spent on my training was well spent indeed; it had given me a whole new approach and outlook to life.

Once my treatment was over I started to tell everyone that I had had breast cancer and, when asked, how I had approached it. Many friends, colleagues and family were shocked. Some gave me the reaction of "I'm so sorry, are you okay now?" and others were really interested in, and inspired by, what I had done. Those are the ones who told me I had to write this book. Amazingly some therapist colleagues have taken me to one side and told me that I'm obviously not over it as I keep talking to people about it. I should really just let it go now and never mention it again, I shouldn't hang on to it! Yet more subliminal suggestions being given by people who *should* know better.

Cancer seems to be a word people find hard to utter. They hedge around it, hint at it. Now when I see people they will ask, "How are you?"

I answer as I always have, not even thinking of the breast cancer I had, "I'm fine, thank you."

This usually brings a kind of doubtful, questioning look with "No, you know... how are you *really?*" It's at that point I realise they are not referring to how I feel right now but to my encounter with cancer.

Cancer affects a huge number of people and a common impression appears to be that we lose more people to it than we save. I was involved in a conversation about cancer with a friend who didn't know I was going through treatment and they stated: "I don't know of anyone who has ever survived cancer." At the time I smiled inwardly and said nothing.

A few months ago I reminded her of the conversation and told her, "Now you *do* know a cancer survivor. You're looking at her."

In that moment I could see that I had changed her belief, her view and her fear of cancer. She smiled, gave me a huge hug and said, "Thank you." I knew exactly what she meant by those two simple words.

So will I stop telling people I had cancer? Obviously not, or I wouldn't have written this book.

The incidence of breast cancer may be increasing but the fact is that in the UK *over three-quarters* of women who have been diagnosed with it survive for *at least* ten years, and the outlook continues to improve. This information is easily available via Cancer Research UK, yet many people firmly believe the survival rates to be much worse. My wish would be to ensure that there is a balanced view so that when someone is told they have "the big C" the automatic fall-back thought is not a negative one but a more positive one. The overriding belief must be that it can be cured, no matter what stage it is at. There are many cases where people have recovered even when they've been told it was terminal. In fact, having just read

138

those sentences, I would like to see an "unbalanced" view in **favour** of people surviving cancer. People diagnosed would then approach it from a much stronger, more hopeful, positive angle and we all know how powerful the mind can be. Family and friends would also naturally be giving out positive vibes rather than "trying to be strong."

Unfortunately there are no statistics available looking at precisely *how* the survivors survived. Was it just through mainstream medical treatment? Was it through using other techniques, or a combination? I would love to see serious research focused on what those people who "cured" it did differently. What were they thinking, how did they approach it, what did they change, what did they do that others didn't? We shouldn't simply ignore them or put it down to a one-off, luck or a fluke. We should research them and study them in depth, instead of simply filing away their notes never to be seen again, for surely some of the answers to getting rid of cancer lie with them.

For me the NHS system worked. I applaud the medical staff I encountered during my treatment. On the whole they carried out their duties and applied their skills efficiently and with professionalism. I am grateful to them and pleased to have them on *MY* team, but it must be said that none of them showed more than a passing interest in what *I* was doing to help *myself.* Nobody took any notes, nobody made a record of what *I* did at any stage. I will go down as a survivor – that's all – but I am in no doubt that what *I* did was just as important as what *they* did.

CHAPTER 17

Techniques

In this chapter I will be sharing with you the techniques I used to deal with my cancer and its treatment. They are drawn from the worlds of Neuro-Linguistic Programming (NLP), Thought Field Therapy (TFT) and Reality Transurfing. Plus there are techniques where I combined a whole mixture of things that worked for me, and my belief system. So feel free to adapt, alter, develop, even make up ones that will work for you. Have fun, let your imagination run wild – in a *positive* way!

Visualisation

It is important to understand exactly what you are expecting when we talk about visualisation. So many people struggle with it, swear they can't do it and that they get a feeling first. Actually they will have seen the picture first, however briefly, and it is the picture that then brings the feeling.

The expectation of a lot of people is that when you visualise something it is as clear and focused as if you were looking at a film or photograph. This may well be the case for some people but in my experience it is much more like an *impression* of a film or photograph. One way to check out what your visualisation looks or feels like is to think of some basic everyday things. Describe your lounge. What colour is your car interior? What side is your fridge door handle on? In order to be able to answer those questions you will have had to picture your lounge, car interior or fridge door. That is what your visualisation looks like for you. Some of you may still be arguing that you could answer those questions because you "just knew the answers". Well, in that case ask some harder questions.

Next you need to decide what would work for you in whatever situation you are in. Think about the outcome that you want to achieve and what you would need to achieve it. As you know, for me it wasn't about "fighting and killing" the cancer cells but about loving them like I do all my other cells and changing them, getting them "back in line". I needed something that would fit with my belief system and was powerful for me as well as easy to imagine. You need to find something that fits with your belief system.

Plenty of people will give you suggestions about what you *should* be imagining. With cancer that usually involves doing battle with the cancer cells, fighting and destroying them, but this is about *YOU* and what works for *YOU*. Remember you can use lots of different visualisations for different parts of your treatment. Simply think about what it is you want to change or counteract and find an appropriate answer that you can then visualise.

After my treatment had been completed I was talking to someone who had just started their chemotherapy and was struggling with it. They had been visualising "attacking the aliens with an enormous armoury". For their chemotherapy they saw it as poison (which of course it is) flowing through their body, again with the purpose to poison and kill all their cells. A tip here is to be careful what you tell yourself and be *very* specific. They really didn't mean *all* their cells, only the cancerous ones. After their chemotherapy treatments they had felt quite ill. We talked about it for a while, what they wanted to achieve and how they wanted to feel. They decided they wanted to change their visualisation that had been suggested by others and see the chemotherapy drugs as a clear mountain stream, flowing into a muddy, dirty river that needed cleansing. As the stream joined the river it washed away all the dirt and sludge leaving a much cleaner, calmer river behind. They felt this was also a far more relaxing visualisation and not such hard work or anywhere near as stressful to do.

There is now a lot of research into how visualisation and what you think literally changes the chemicals produced in the brain and as a result the physiological impact on the body. An excellent book for finding out more behind how our thoughts affect our body is 'How Your Mind Can Heal Your Body' by Dr David Hamilton.

This longer than usually allowed extract has been reproduced with the very kind permission of **Dr David Hamilton.**

"As part of the brain-changing process, thoughts produce chemicals in the brain. Many are known as neurotransmitters. You may have heard of serotonin and dopamine, which are two well known neurotransmitters.

When we think thoughts, neurotransmitters are released from the branch of one neuron and make their way to the tip of a branch of another. This produces a bolt of electricity and is what is known as neuron 'firing'. When we repeat a thought several times, an additional chemical (protein) is stimulated and makes its way to the centre of the neuron (the nucleus), where it finds DNA. It then activates (switches on) several genes of DNA, which make the substances (proteins) that produce new branches (connections) between the neurons. In this way, repeating a thought produces new connections between neurons and is how the brain changes with our thoughts and experiences.

> *The process is rapid. Genes are activated within a few minutes and a single neuron may gain thousands of new branches in a very short time. One of the significant things to note here is that the genes have been activated by a state of mind within minutes. This is mind over matter rapidly taking place at the genetic level and has a key role to play in many so-called miraculous healings.*
>
> *Another type of chemical, known as a neuropeptide, is also produced in the brain."*
>
> *"Many neuropeptides don't just hang a round in the brain. Many are released into the bloodstream and travel throughout the body where they carry out important roles. Thus, in a link between mind and body, our thoughts and emotions produce neuropeptides and affect the whole body."*

Change that Film*

Concentrate on the film of your diagnosis that you are running in your head and if it is negative or scary in *even the smallest way* then you should change it. This will help:

In your mind imagine walking into a cinema and sitting down in the middle of the front row.

Then imagine floating up out of your body into the projection room at the back of the cinema so that now you can see the back of your head watching the screen.

Imagine that up on the screen is a coloured slide of the moment you received your diagnosis. Staying in the projection room, watch yourself in the cinema, watching the screen as you start the film that you have been running since your diagnosis, through to what you see as the outcome. Be aware of how you are feeling, what you are seeing and what you are hearing as you watch the film. Ask yourself if this is how you want things to go. (My film was a very positive one and absolutely how I wanted things to go.) However if the answer is no, this is *not* how you want things to go, then at the end of the film freeze-frame it into a still slide. Now drain all the colour out and turn it into black and white.. Run the movie backwards at triple speed or even faster whilst circus music or 'Benny Hill'-type music is playing.

When you get back to the beginning of the movie freeze-frame it. White out the screen, go to the end of the film and repeat the process several times.

Finally when you have reached the freeze-frame at the beginning and you feel differently about the film, return to your seat in the front row of the cinema. Then white out the whole screen completely.

Next decide on how you would like the story in the film to evolve in a really positive way. Make sure the film is in full-blown technicolor (and nowadays it could also be 3D). Step into the film so you are seeing everything with your own eyes, hearing everything with your own ears as if you were there, and feeling really good. Then press the play button and let the film run way into the future. Play it again and again and again.

*This NLP technique has been adapted from Dr Richard Bandler's Fast Phobia Cure.

Circles of Confidence / Strength / Power

Imagine a time when you were extremely confident and knew beyond a shadow of a doubt that you were going to have a positive outcome about something. See everything you saw, feel everything you felt and hear everything you heard.

Now give that feeling a colour, imagine a circle of that colour in front of you and another in front of that one and then another, and so on, out in front of you.

Step into that first circle and feel the colour moving up through your legs, body and head, flooding you with confidence, strength and power. Every step you take from now on is into a coloured circle of confidence, strength and power, helping you to build a positive belief about your outcome.

Change that Voice*

What you say to yourself unconsciously (otherwise known as thinking) has a conscious impact on how you feel, behave and react. In reality the most important person you will ever talk to is *you*. Because what most of us never realise is that what you say to yourself has a massive impact on the way you feel.

Close your eyes, now listen to that internal voice in your head telling you how scary and terrible things are going to be – whether it is some sort of operation or following a diagnosis of cancer or other disease.

You've probably never noticed before but the voice will be talking to you from one particular place inside your head. If you were to point to the location of that voice in your head where would it be? Is it talking to you from the front or back of your head? Maybe it's on the left, maybe the right? What sort of tone does it have?

When you think about your operation or illness the negative voice will be heard loud and clear. Notice what you are feeling while you are listening to the voice. Are you feeling positive and upbeat? Chances are it is making you feel frightened, worried and unhappy, even angry about your situation. *By turning that voice off you can turn off the negative feelings that come with it.*

Now close your eyes and say some positive things to yourself not related to your condition. Maybe a time when you were really happy or a situation that made you laugh

145

really hard. Locate the position of that voice in your head. Is it in the same place or different? For the majority of people it will be in a different place in their head. Some of my clients have a problem locating the voice that says "good things" to them and have to work at finding it. It is there, you may have to listen harder to hear it but once located, focus on it, give it your full attention.

Once you have located the voices involved in your internal dialogue there are several ways in which you can stop the negative voice:

Shut the F**K Up!
Locate your positive voice and with that voice simply shout at the negative voice to "SHUT UP, SHUT UP, JUST SHUT UP WILL YOU!" If you want to add an expletive feel free – it's your voice and it's in your head so no one else can hear you! Some people find it easier to do if they give the negative voice a name, then they can shout at it with added feeling!

Change the Tone...
The tone in which something is said can change the way you feel about it. For example something as simple as "Thank you" can be said in a sarcastic tone, friendly tone, loving tone, aggressive tone – each causing a different reaction as to how we feel.

What tone of voice makes you smile? What sort of voice can't you take seriously? Mickey Mouse? Peter Kay? Someone you know? A high, squeaky voice? Find that negative voice in your head now, as it is talking, and change the tone, make it as funny as you can. How much power does that voice have now on the way you feel about your phobia?

Switch it Off...
If I asked you to describe a switch to turn something off what sort would it be? Would it be like a light switch, a pull switch, a big lever, a big dial, a fader or perhaps a keypad that you press, like on a remote control? To be able

to tell me you will have made a picture of one in your mind. Whichever switch you saw, imagine making it bigger, bigger, *even bigger!* Now locate that negative voice again, get it to say all those scary, negative things to you about your situation and then flick that switch in your head to switch it off. Now turn up the volume on the positive voice so you can hear it reinforcing all the positive, confident things you need to make you feel calm, relaxed and confident about your condition. Notice how the feelings in your body change and how you are now reacting towards what was previously a frightening situation or diagnosis.

Push it Away...
Another way of 'quietening' that negative voice is to simply push it so far away from you that you can't hear it anymore. Imagine that negative voice is talking to you from the end of your thumb, at the end of your out stretched arm. Yes, go on – stretch out your arm and imagine your thumb talking to you in that negative voice. If you like, change it into that silly tone. How powerful an effect is it having on you now? Okay, now imagine it talking to you from across the room… across the street… Can you still hear it? Push it even further away. Can you even be bothered to strain your ears to hear it? So now listen to your positive voice giving you encouragement and reinforcing your new belief about a good outcome.

*This NLP technique is reproduced with the written permission of Dr Richard Bandler

Thought Field Therapy

TFT is a non-invasive, drug-free procedure that you can use to treat yourself to conquer emotional stress and many of life's problems. It is sometimes called *tapping* and involves literally tapping with your fingers into the body's energy with specific information to allow healing whilst concentrating on the problem.

It works on the body's own energy field, using precise and defined tapping sequences on specific Energy Meridian Points, similar to those used in acupuncture. TFT offers dynamic results in a very short space of time and can be incredibly effective in helping with anxiety, stress, phobias, fears, trauma, OCD, guilt, anger, addictive urges and physical pain, as well as numerous other problems. Many of the symptoms people experience are caused by "Individual Energy Toxins" (IETs). Once these are identified and avoided people gain relief from their problems. The effects of a TFT treatment can be virtually instantaneous and occur without months of expensive therapy or drugs. Many TFT users experience almost immediate relief and the best bit is that you can treat yourself whenever you need to! It doesn't remove the memory, you will still remember events, but what is *does* do is take away the emotional negativity associated with an event.

In TFT you can tap either side of the body and it doesn't matter if you cross over during the sequence, e.g. under the eye on the left side, under the arm on the right. It is the sequence of points that matters. It is important to remember that with TFT whatever you are thinking about is what you will be treating.

I've included a couple of sequences: one for getting rid of traumas and another one for stress and anxiety.

When tapping make sure you tap hard enough so that you can feel it but not so hard as to give yourself a bruise!

Tapping Points

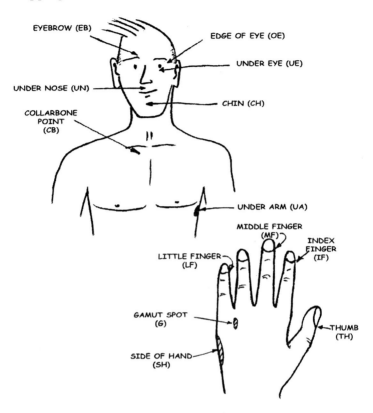

*Sequence for clearing a trauma***

Focus on the event that caused the trauma (perhaps it was the original diagnosis or when you discovered a lump). Now rate how you feel about it on a scale from 1 – 10 with 10 being the highest. (This is important as it will be the indicator of how much you have reduced your fear.) On a scale of 1 – 10 how strong is your fear/anxiety associated with that event? Thinking about that event, take two fingers (of either hand) and:

Tap on the side at the end of your Index Finger (IF) x 10

Then tap the side of one of your hands into the palm of the other (as if you were doing a karate chop).
SH x 10

Keep thinking about that event and tap the following points approximately 5 times:

Inside edge of the eyebrow (EB)
Under the eye (UE)
Under the arm (UA)
On the collarbone point (CB) (approximately 3-4cms from the 'notch' in the middle and 3-4cms below the collarbone)

Now whilst continually tapping the back of the other hand on the knuckles between the ring finger and little finger (Gamut spot) and without moving your head:

Close your eyes
Open your eyes
Look down to one side
Look down to the other
Hum a couple of bars of a tune out loud (it must be hum, not sing!)
Count to 5 out loud
Hum a couple of bars again

Now go back and tap:

Eyebrow (EB)
Under the eye (UE)
Under the Arm (UA)
Collarbone point (CB)

Stop tapping and focus on the event again. What number is it now? It should be lower. Repeat the sequence until it has come down to zero.

Note: if there is more than one incident that contributed to the onset of the trauma (finding the lump may be one, having it confirmed by the consultant may be another) treat each one separately.

When the anxiety about the trauma has diminished then use one of the following sequences:

Sequence to reduce and clear any fear, stress and anxiety**
Focus on your fear/stress/anxiety. Now rate its level on a scale from 1 – 10 with 10 being the highest. (This is important as it will be the indicator of how much you have reduced your fear.) On a scale of 1 – 10 how strong is your fear/stress/anxiety?

    Thinking about that fear/ stress/anxiety take 2 fingers (of either hand) and:
Tap on the side at the end of your Index Finger (IF) x 10
Then tap the side of one of your hands into the palm of the other (as if you were doing a karate chop)
SH x 10

Keep thinking about your fear/stress/anxiety and tap the following points approximately 5 times:

Under the eye (UE)
Under the arm (UA)
On the collarbone point (CB) (approximately 3-4cms from the 'notch' in the middle and 3-4cms below the collarbone)

Now whilst continually tapping the back of the other hand on the knuckles between the ring finger and little finger (Gamut spot) and without moving your head:

Close your eyes
Open your eyes
Look down to one side

151

Look down to the other
Hum a couple of bars of a tune out loud (it must be hum, not sing!)
Count to 5 out loud
Hum a couple of bars again

Now go back and tap:

Under the eye (UE)
Under the Arm (UA)
Collarbone point (CB)
Stop tapping and focus on the fear/stress/anxiety again. What number is it now? It should be lower. Repeat the sequence until it is down to zero.

**These sequences are reproduced with the written permission of Dr Roger Callahan Techniques.

What if it still hasn't gone after repeating the sequences?
There are a couple of reasons why a sequence may not work. During his discovery and research of TFT, its founder Dr Callahan discovered that people can suffer from what he called *reversals* at different levels during the treatment. If a person is "reversed" this can have the effect of blocking the treatment. By finding and correcting the reversals at the different levels, easily done by a good practitioner, the treatment will work more often than not. If it still isn't effective then IETs could be to blame for blocking the treatment. Remember they are *individual* so different for everyone. A fully trained TFT therapist would be able to identify very quickly your IETs as well as dealing with any reversals.

As you know from reading this book, I avoided all my IETs, not just because I wanted tapping sequences to work but because I wanted to give my body as much help as possible in healing me. By removing my IETs my body didn't have to work on clearing those on top of everything else, it could just work on what it really needed to.

Avoiding my IETs as much as possible is a way of life to me now, helping my body function at its best.

CHAPTER 18

Recipes

The following recipes have come from various sources: friends, family, magazines, books, the internet and from my own experimenting.

So thank you to the people who originally came up with them and who I've been unable to acknowledge as I don't know who they are. Since I started my treatment I've become so much more aware of fantastic-tasting recipes that are healthy. As a result we as a family are now eating healthily.

I'm also pleased to say that my friend Matt Burgess shared with me that what I'd done, and the food I was eating, had inspired him to make a lifestyle change. He altered his diet, but didn't go *on a diet*, started exercising and has lost over three stone (19kg) in weight in five months and is still losing it. The day before writing this I was texting him the chocolate balls recipe as he fancied a treat, and we were talking about what he's achieved and how he feels.

He texted, "I would tell the world if I could. I also get the urge to pull burgers out of the hands of fat people and scream at them!!!!! There is no need to eat that s**t!" When I reminded him that he used to be one of them, he texted back, "Yes and I remember. I cringe now thinking about it. A past I would rather forget but now I use it to remind myself about the dangers of not caring".

If I've helped just one of my friends to care about themselves and live a healthier, longer life then I'm happy.

I hope you are inspired to try some of these recipes and search out new ways of preparing food.

Quinoa Porridge (serves 4)

Ingredients
>200g (2 cups) quinoa flakes
>475ml (2cups) goats milk (or any nut milk)
>750ml (3 cups) water
>1 cinnamon stick (optional)

Method

Place the quinoa flakes, cinnamon stick, 250ml (1 cup) of milk and 475ml (2 cups) of water in a pan. Stir continuously over a medium heat for 2-3 minutes, add the remaining water and stir for another 2 minutes, until piping hot.

Heat the remaining milk in a separate pan.

Spoon the porridge into 4 bowls, pour over hot milk and serve sprinkled with fresh fruit of your choice – pomegranate seeds are recommended.

You can substitute all sorts of things in this recipe. My personal favourite is adding vanilla essence in the pan, liberal sprinkling cinnamon over it and a dollop of goat's yogurt and maple syrup instead of the hot milk in the bowl.

Gill's Quinoa Granola

Ingredients
>¼ cup of liquid (melted) coconut oil
>¼ cup good quality maple syrup (I use less as I prefer it not so sweet)
>1 ½ cups of quinoa flakes
>¼ cup ground almonds (optional)
>1 tbsp cinnamon (optional)
>Coarse sea salt

Optional Additions
Add any type of nuts, seeds or dried fruit you fancy.

Method

Pre-heat the oven to 400F / 200C.

Whisk together the melted coconut oil and maple syrup in a large mixing bowl and add the quinoa flakes, ground almonds and cinnamon, stirring to combine thoroughly. Evenly spread the quinoa mixture on a baking sheet lined with greaseproof paper (parchment) and sprinkle with a pinch of salt. Roast stirring now and then, until the flakes are dried and a lovely golden brown, about 25 minutes. Let the quinoa granola cool completely before mixing with the remaining ingredients of your choice. Store in an airtight container for 2 weeks.

Serve with a bit of fresh fruit, goat's yogurt or almond milk. Alternatively eat as a healthy snack.

Gill's 'American Style' Quinoa Pancakes

Ingredients

      150g quinoa flour
      1 tbs baking powder
      generous pinch of salt
      1 tsp xylitol
      60g coconut oil (or shortening)
      1 cup of milk (any type of milk)
      1 egg

Method

Mix the quinoa flour, baking powder, salt and xylitol together then rub in the coconut oil. Beat the egg and milk together and then add to the dry ingredients. Beat well until the mixture is a thick running consistency.

Melt some oil in a frying pan. Place approximately a ladle full of the mixture into the frying pan. When cooked on one side flip the pancake over and finish cooking. Serve with whatever takes your fancy.

Quinoa, herb & pomegranate salad
Serves 2, ready in 20 minutes

Ingredients

> 150g quinoa
> ½ vegetable stock cube
> 75g pine nuts
> 1 pomegranate, seeds removed
> small handful mint, chopped
> small handful coriander, chopped
> 1 lime, juiced
> extra-virgin olive oil

Method

Cook the quinoa according to pack instructions adding the vegetable stock to the cooking water. Leave to cool then break up with a fork.

Meanwhile, toast the pine nuts in a dry frying pan until lightly golden. Mix pine nuts, pomegranate seeds, herbs, lime juice and 4tbsp oil through the quinoa.

Recipe extra

Add chopped dried apricots instead of the pomegranate. Or try adding some cooked shredded chicken.

Spicy vegetable & quinoa laksa

Ingredients

      I onion sliced
      4 tbsp vegetarian korma or madras curry paste
      I litre goat's mlik
      750g frozen (or fresh cooked) mixed vegetables
      175g quinoa, rinsed

Method

Simmer the onion and the curry paste with a splash of water for 5 mins in a large saucepan, stirring from time to time. Heat the goat's milk.

Add the vegetables and quinoa, then stir in the milk. Bring to the boil, simmer gently for 10 mins until the quinoa is cooked. Check seasoning.

Cajun Sweet Potato Wedges

Ingredients

      3 sweet potatoes peeled and cut into large wedges
      2 tbsp olive oil or melted coconut oil
      Cajun spice mix to taste

Method

Place the sweet potato wedges in a large bowl with the olive oil and Cajun spice mix to taste, and toss well to coat thoroughly.

Transfer to a baking tray and cook in a preheated oven, 160°C/325°F/gas mark 3, for 30 minutes or until golden brown.

Desserts – YUM!

Raw Chocolate Ganache Tart
(You can use half quantities for a smaller tart)

Ingredients for the base
> 300g pecans or almonds
> 1 tsp pink Himalayan salt, or any other good-quality salt
> 200g medjool dates (must be medjool dates as they are nice and sticky)

For the filling
> 4 medium sized ripe avocados
> 150g virgin coconut oil
> 2 vanilla pods, seeds only
> 200g raw cacao powder (cocoa powder will also work)
> Pinch of salt
> 200g maple syrup to taste

Method

In a food processor, blend the pecans or almonds (if possible, soak them for around 6 hours and then dehydrate them first. The soaking releases the enzyme inhibitors and makes them easier to digest.) Add the salt and medjool dates and blend until you have a 'dough', or until the mix forms a ball.

Press this mixture into the bottom of a mould. Cover in cling film and leave to harden in the freezer until you are ready to pour on the filling.

Silicone moulds are best as they are freezer-safe and it's easy to get the tart out once it has set. However I have used a loose-bottom sandwich tin, but you need be careful taking it out of the freezer with bare hands!

For the filling, blend everything together until smooth, then pour on to the base.

Set in the freezer for 1 hour, then it should be firm enough to slice up. Top with fresh berries, edible flowers, a dusting of cacao powder, whatever takes your fancy and looks pretty!

Note: As yet I've not soaked the nuts as I've always been in a hurry to make it. I wouldn't say the filling pours out as it's thick and lovely and sticky. I've had to spoon it out and then of course just had to lick the spoon clean when I've finished!

Fruit Crumble Topping

Ingredients

    4tbsp good quality maple syrup
    1 cup ground almonds
    1 cup quinoa flakes
    Pinch of fine sea salt
    1 tsp ground cinnamon
    4tbsp extra virgin coconut oil (melted)
    alternatively you can use olive oil.

Method

Mix the almond meal, quinoa flakes, salt and cinnamon in a large bowl. Add the maple syrup and coconut oil and mix until just combined. Crumble the mixture over some prepared fruit of your choice and bake until the topping is browned. 20 to 25 minutes.

Raw Chocolate Mousse

Ingredients

>1 ripe avocado
>1 ripe banana
>3 dessert spoons of maple syrup
>3 dessert spoons of cacao (or cocoa powder)
>A dash of pure vanilla essence
>A pinch of salt
>Cacao nibs for topping

Method

Place all the ingredients into a regular blender and blitz until creamy and smooth. (If you don't have a blender then it can be made by mashing and mixing the ingredients together in a bowl.)

Hold back on some of the maple syrup to finish off, based on your sweet preference. I find two dessert spoonfuls are sweet enough.

Spoon in separate serving glasses and top with cacao nibs. Makes enough for two servings. Increase quantities to achieve more servings.

Sweet Potato Chocolate Brownies

Ingredients
> 125g (4oz/generous ¾ cup) rice flour
> 75g (3oz/ ¾ cup) raw cacao powder
> ¼ tsp baking powder
> 175g (6oz) sweet potato, cooked and mashed to a puree
> 250g (8oz / scant ¾ cup) date syrup
> 175g (6oz / scant ¾ cup) goat's butter, melted
> 1 egg
> ¼ tsp vanilla extract

Method

Preheat the oven to 180c / 350f / gas mark 4

Sift the rice flour, cacao powder and baking powder into a bowl.

Place the sweet potato puree, date syrup, melted butter, egg and vanilla extract in another bowl and mix together well. Then stir in the dry ingredients.

Pour the brownie mixture into a rectangular cake tin lined with baking parchment and bake for 20 – 25 minutes, until set on top but gooey in the middle. Cool in the tin, then cut into pieces. Can be served hot or cold.

Raw Caramel Slice (Makes 16 big slices)

Ingredients

Base

½ cup Medjool dates
1 ½ cups almonds
1 tsp vanilla essence

Caramel

½ cup tahini
½ cup maple syrup
¼ cup coconut oil
1 tsp vanilla essence
Large pinch Himalayan salt

Chocolate topping

3-4 tbsp raw cacao
1 tsp carob powder
3-4 tbsp coconut sugar or agave syrup
½ cup coconut oil

Method

Grind dates and almonds in blender or food processor. Add vanilla until sticky and then press into rectangular dish greased in coconut oil.

Blend caramel ingredients together and pour over biscuit base and set in the freezer for 20 minutes.

While slice is setting, melt coconut oil for chocolate crunch topping and then add all other ingredients and stir well. Let cool for 5 minutes and then pour topping over slice and place back in freezer to set again.

Cut into small squares to serve.

Treats!

Chocolate Coconut Balls (makes 12)

Ingredients
>10 fresh dates, pitted
>50g raw cacao powder
>25g raw almonds
>200g coconut flakes
>30g maple syrup
>2 tbsp coconut oil
>1 tsp xylitol
>2 tbsp water

Method

Preheat the oven to 180°C/350°F/gas mark 4
Mix the dates, cacao powder and almonds in a blender or food processor for about 1 minute to make a sticky, chunky paste. Add the remaining ingredients and blend to a rough consistency.

Transfer the mixture to a bowl, divide it into 12 pieces and roll into balls. Place them on a baking tray lined with baking parchment and bake for 10 minutes. Allow to cool.

Raw Mango Coconut Balls (Makes 20)

Ingredients

      250g dessicated coconut (dry, unsweetened)
      200g dried unsweetened, unsulphured mango (organic if possible) soaked in water for 30 minutes and drained
      40g maple syrup
      8 tbsp coconut oil
      2 tsp freshly grated lemon zest

Method

Place 225g of the coconut in a food processor with the mango, maple syrup, coconut oil and lemon zest and pulse until the mixture comes together. Transfer this to a bowl.

Put the remaining coconut in a separate bowl. Form the mixture into small balls and coat them in coconut.

Freeze the coconut balls for 20 minutes on a baking tray lined with parchment paper. Store in an airtight container in the refrigerator.

BIBLIOGRAPHY

Love, Medicine and Miracles, Bernie Siegel, UK: Rider, 1999

Reality Transurfing, 1. The Space of Variations, Vadim Zeland, O Books, 2008

Reality Transurfing, 2. A Rustle of Mornign Stars, Vadim Zeland, O Books, 2008

Reality Transurfing, 3. Forward to the Past, Vadim Zeland, O Books, 2008

Reality Transurfing, 4. Ruling Reality, Vadim Zeland, O Books, 2012

Reality Transurfing, 5. Apples Fall to the Sky, Vadim Zeland, O Books, 2012

The Field, Lynne McTaggart, Harper Collins, 2003

Food is Better Medicine than Drugs, Patrick Holford & Jerome Burn. Piatkus Books, 2006

The Disease Delusion, Dr. Jeffrey S. Bland Harper Collins 2014

Tapping the Healer Within, Roger Callahan, Piatkus Books, 2008

You Can Have What You Want, Michael Neill, Hay House, 2006

How Your Mind Can Heal Your Body, Dr David R. Hamilton Phd, Hay House 2012

And NLP from any book by Dr Richard Bandler or Paul McKenna.

REFERENCES

1. Goodwin PJ, Ennis M, Pritchard KI, Trudeau ME, Koo J, Madarnas Y, Hartwick W, Hoffman B, Hood N. Fasting Insulin and Outcome in Early-Stage Breast Cancer: Results of a Prospective Cohort Study. *J Clin Oncol*. 2002;20:42-51.

2. Goodwin PJ, Ennis M, Pritchard KI, Trudeau ME, Koo J, Hartwick W, Hoffman B, Hood N. Insulin-like growth factor binding proteins 1 and 3 and breast cancer outcomes. *Breast Cancer Res Treat*. 2002;74:65-76.

3. Sauter ER, Chervoneva I, Diamandis A, Khosravi JM, Litwin S, Diamandis EP. Prostate-specific antigen and insulin-like growth factor binding protein-3 in nipple aspirate fluid are associated with breast cancer. *Cancer Detect Prev*. 2002;26:149-157.

4. Baron JA, Weiderpass E, Newcomb PA, Stampfer M, Titus-Ernstoff L, Egan KM, Greenberg ER. Metabolic disorders and breast cancer risk. *Cancer Causes Control*. 2001;12:875-880.

5. Augustin LS, Dal Maso L, La Vecchia C, Parpinel M, Negri E, Vaccarella S, Kendall CW, Jenkins DJ, Francesch S. Dietary glycemic index and glycemic load, and breast cancer risk: A case-control study. *Ann Oncol*. 2001;12:1533-1538.

6. Toniolo P, Bruning PF, Akhmedkhanov A, Bonfrer JMG, Koenig KL, Lukanova A, Shore RE, Zeleniuch-Jacquotte A. Serum insulin-like growth factor-I and breast cancer. *Int J Cancer*. 2000;88:828-832.

Lightning Source UK Ltd.
Milton Keynes UK
UKOW04f1224241115

263403UK00002B/24/P